HISTORIC WHITHORN

*CHAPEL OF THE ISLE,
ISLE OF WHITHORN, WIGTONSHIRE.
VIEW LOOKING S.W. (OCT. 1887)*

HISTORIC WHITHORN

Archaeology and development

R D Oram
P F Martin
C A McKean
T Neighbour

THE SCOTTISH BURGH SURVEY

Published by the Council for British Archaeology and Historic Scotland
First published in 2010

Copyright © 2010 Historic Scotland

The moral right of the authors has been asserted.

British Library Cataloguing in Publication Data

A catalogue for this book is available from the British Library

Edited by Catrina Appleby, CBA and Mark Watson, Historic Scotland

Page design and typesetting by Carnegie Publishing Ltd

Printing and binding: Information Press, Oxford

ISBN: 978-1-902771-82-3

Council for British Archaeology
St Mary's House,
66 Bootham,
York YO30 7BZ
www.britarch.ac.uk

Historic Scotland
Longmore House
Salisbury Place
Edinburgh
EH9 1SH
Tel. 0131 668 8600
Fax. 0131 668 8669
www.historic-scotland.gov.uk

All rights are reserved. No part of this publication may be reproduced, stored in a retrieval system, transmitted or utilised in any form or by any means electronic, mechanical or by photocopying, recording or otherwise, without the written permission of Historic Scotland.

Front cover: Whithorn from the air, looking west (Crown copyright: RCAHMS)

Insets: Early medieval carved stones found at Whithorn (Crown copyright: Historic Scotland); the burgh seal, which appears to be a secularised version of the seal of the priory. It depicts St Ninian in secular dress, with chains or manacles to either side – items traditionally associated with Ninian in medieval images

Half-title page: Drawing by General Pitt-Rivers of the chapel at Isle of Whithorn (Crown copyright: Historic Scotland)

Contents

Illustrations

Maps

Tables & Graphs

Abbreviations

CRB	*Records of the Convention of the Royal Burghs of Scotland,* vol i, 1295–1597 (Edinburgh, 1866), vol ii, 1597–1614 (Edinburgh, 1870), vol iii, 1614–76 (Edinburgh, 1878), vol iv, 1677–1711 (Edinburgh, 1880)
CSP	*Calendar of State Papers Relating to Scotland and Mary, Queen of Scots 1547–1603,* ed J Bain and others (Edinburgh, 1898–)
DES	*Discovery and Excavation in Scotland*
ER	*The Exchequer Rolls of Scotland,* eds J Stuart *et al* (Edinburgh, 1878–1908)
Historians of York	*Historians of the Church of York and Its Archbishops,* ed J Raine, 2 vols (London, 1869–94)
NMRS	National Monuments Record of Scotland
NSA	*The New Statistical Account of Scotland* (Edinburgh, 1845), 'Parish of Whithorn', Rev Christopher Nicholson, 1839
OSA	*The Statistical Account of Scotland 1791–1799, vol 5, Stewartry of Kirkcudbright and Wigtownshire,* new edition I R Grant and D J Withrington (eds) (Wakefield, 1983), 'Parish of Whithorn', Rev Isaac Davidson, 1794
PSAS	*Proceedings of the Society of Antiquaries of Scotland*
RCAHMS	Royal Commission on the Ancient and Historical Monuments of Scotland
Reg. Gray	*Register of Walter Gray, Lord Archbishop of York* (Surtees Society, 1870)
Reg. Romeyn	*Register of John le Romeyn, Lord Archbishop of York* (Surtees Society, 1913–16)
RMS	*Registrum Magni Sigilli Regum Scotorum*
RPC	*Register of the Privy Council of Scotland*
RPS	*Register of the Privy Seal*
RRS	*Regesta Regum Scotorum*
SHS	Scottish History Society
TA	*Accounts of the Lord High Treasurer of Scotland*
TDGNHAS	*Transactions of the Dumfries & Galloway Natural History and Archaeological Society*
Watt, *Fasti*	*Fasti Ecclesiae Scoticanae Medii Aevi ad Annum 1638,* ed D E R Watt (Scottish Record Society, 1969)
Wigtownshire Chrs	*Wigtownshire Charters,* ed R C Reid (SHS, 1960)

Acknowledgements

As ever, the staff of the libraries and archives we visited, or which have supplied illustrations, have been friendly and helpful. These include the National Library of Scotland and the National Archives of Scotland. We are grateful for permission to reproduce images from the British Library, the Royal Commission on the Ancient and Historical Monuments of Scotland, the National Museums of Scotland and the National Archives of Scotland, besides those of Historic Scotland.

Our great thanks go to the people of Whithorn for their support during the preparation of this report, especially to Janet Butterworth at the Whithorn Trust for supplying access to interim and draft publications relating to the excavations around the priory, and to the Friends of the Whithorn Trust who provided us with much valuable information during our field visit. Our thanks go also to Mr John Pickin of Stranraer Museum for help with various questions and particularly for access to the list of monumental inscriptions, and Mr Andrew Nicholson of Dumfries and Galloway Council for his generous assistance in obtaining copies of the watching brief reports and unpublished archaeological excavation reports. Mr Ray Chadburn's generous permission to use his draft report on quarry sources for building stone used at Dundrennan Abbey and Whithorn Priory was greatly appreciated. Thank you, also, to the Scoulars at the Steam Packet Inn in Isle of Whithorn for both their excellent hospitality and their detailed local knowledge.

Preface: Use of the Burgh Survey

Continued evolution is the essence of urban life. Change is inevitable in towns and is what gives them their vitality. Yet it is the imprint of history that gives localities their distinctive character. Conservation is a matter of ensuring that the qualities that dcfine a place are maintained while change continues to happen. Managing change requires an understanding of that character.

The Scottish Burgh Survey is a guide to the archaeological resource in towns, published by Historic Scotland and the Council for British Archaeology. It helps to influence decision-makers and to set the research agenda on questions that may be answered by archaeology where development occurs. Publications in the latest series may be found at http://www.britarch.ac.uk/pubs/latest.html.

This third series of Burgh Surveys is intended to furnish local authorities, developers and residents with reliable information to help manage the archaeology and historic environment of Scotland's urban centres. It offers comprehensive and consistent base-line information against which research, regeneration and land use planning objectives may be set. It also guides the general reader in researching the rich history and archaeology of Scotland's historic burghs.

The first points of reference in this volume for local authorities to use in the planning process should be the character maps (**maps 11 & 13**), which characterise different parts of Whithorn and Isle of Whithorn and suggest areas of prime archaeological interest. Discoveries may yet be made, however, that will necessitate a reassessment of the state of knowledge of the burgh. As Whithorn is not much larger now than it was in the Middle Ages and as it is set in a landscape of considerable interest, linked to its port at Isle of Whithorn, it would be invidious to single out in a map any parts of the town as free of archaeological interest. Therefore the archaeologically sensitive areas are those defined in the Dumfries and Galloway Council local plan. Map 12 logs archaeological finds made so far in the burgh and a colour-coded map (**map 10** and the **broadsheet**) illustrates phases in its evolution.

Further research into the archaeological potential of a site within a historic town can be gleaned from local and national libraries and archives. The PASTMAP website (http://www.PASTMAP.org.uk) can also be consulted. This interactive website, supported jointly by Historic Scotland and The Royal Commission on the Ancient and Historical Monuments of Scotland, allows searching of data on Scotland's historic environment including the statutorily protected sites, scheduled ancient monuments and listed buildings.

Both this Burgh Survey and the PASTMAP website provide information only. Where development is being considered, advice should be sought in all cases directly from Dumfries & Galloway Council Archaeology Unit, Planning and Environment, Dumfries & Galloway Council, Newall Terrace, Dumfries, DG1 1LW.

Introduction to the Survey

The named authors represent the core of a larger team. Kevin Hicks and Leeanne Whitelaw of CFA Archaeology Ltd produced the maps. Fieldwork was carried out in early March 2006 by Richard Oram, Charles McKean, Paula Martin and Tim Neighbour, with Colin Martin as a companion and extra photographer. The contract was managed for Historic Scotland first by Martin Brann and then Mark Watson.

Before the field trip we carried out desk-based historical and archaeological research, so that we arrived with a set of questions. We explored the town on foot, carrying with us copies of the relevant maps and town plans, then drove around the immediate hinterland. All photographs date from that trip unless otherwise indicated. On our last afternoon we met a group of local people in the Whithorn Story Visitor Centre, presented some of our findings and discussed problems. The feedback we got from this meeting was very useful, and we are grateful to Janet Butterworth at the Whithorn Trust for organising it.

We work as a team, looking for changes in the burgh morphology. We try to spot details and point them out, bouncing ideas off each other. We look at the backs of as many buildings as possible, and try to identify earlier building- and street-lines. Our aim is to understand the morphology of the town, and its various phases of development, within its physical landscape. Existing architectural guides highlight individual buildings, but we aim to see these buildings within their geographical and historical contexts. We prefer to highlight and explain what still survives, rather than lament a vanished past. Our illustrations concentrate on what we saw and judged important or typical.

After the field visit, more research was carried out on the history and archaeology in the light of a better understanding of the burgh, and the sections on architectural styles and building materials developed. The final section on the 'spirit of place' and potential for further research and sympathetic development was the last to be written. The text contributed by four people has been edited and merged into one narrative, though individual voices will inevitably be apparent in places. The original report was presented to Historic Scotland in the summer of 2006, and has developed since then in the light of helpful comments from external readers.

1: Character statement and executive summary

This study addresses the history and archaeology of both the burgh of Whithorn and Isle of Whithorn, as it proved impossible to write about one without the other. The origins of settlement at Whithorn are uncertain, but by the mid-fifth century AD the settlement had a population which included at least some Christians, and a cemetery which appears to have been Christian in character. A monastery may have been founded by the sixth century on the site occupied by the present parish church and priory ruins. This monastery became the focus for a civil settlement of craftsmen and traders, which by the later tenth or early eleventh century had acquired town-like characteristics. In various stages through the twelfth and early thirteenth centuries the monastery was reorganised into the cathedral for the medieval diocese of Whithorn and a convent of Premonstratensian canons. This led, probably in the late thirteenth or early fourteenth century, to the planned relocation of the early settlement around the monastery to a new position on the line of what is now George Street. In the early 1300s, this community was created a burgh of barony for the prior of Whithorn.

The burgh which had grown up alongside the priory prospered by providing services for visitors. Pilgrimage 'was a very profitable activity for the town, which was by far the most cosmopolitan in the south of Scotland', until it was banned in 1581.[1] The burgh consists of one main street (George Street), to the east of the priory, narrowed at both ends but wide for most of its length, providing a very large market-place aligned north-east to south-west. Its size is deceptive, and it may be divided into three parts, each with a particular function: uphill south of the old tolbooth; the central portion between the tolbooth and the Ket burn; and north of the burn.

Not only is the street-line variable, but the boundary along the backlands winds in and out. This is evident on maps from Roy onwards, though it may have been exaggerated since then.[2] One unusual feature of the burgh morphology is that the Ket burn was not used to form a boundary, but crossed the main street at an angle, suggesting that the burgh was laid out along a pre-existing routeway. The result of having to fit around the burn and the priory precinct is that the rigs vary in alignment, and a few once turned at sharp angles to gain access to the burn.[3] The width of the rigs also varies,

FIGURE 1
An example of a narrow house in George Street. Note that although this example does have a chimney on the right as well as the left, there is no formal edge to the roof, as there is on the left (Richard Oram)

with some houses very narrow indeed (**fig 1**), while others are quite spacious (**fig 2**). There seems to be no standard rig width. 'The old royalty was very limited. It comprehended only the present street, and a border of ground behind it, on either side'.[4] It is an unusually tight boundary for a burgh. The present walls between rigs, and on the outer boundary, are drystone and low, resembling field walls rather than the higher mortared backland walls more normally found in burghs. Many pieces of dressed red sandstone survive in these walls, and in some houses there is evidence of reused stones, notably lintels and quoins, probably from the priory (**fig 3**), and window-dressings almost certainly recut from its larger stones.

Whithorn was a burgh of barony, though the prior was given trading rights close to those of a royal burgh, and after the Reformation Whithorn became accepted as *de facto* a royal burgh. However, without the income from pilgrims, and with virtually no common good other than harbour dues from the Isle, the burgh's fortunes soon declined. It was so small that it had no guildry or trade incorporations. Although there were eighteen town councillors, the electorate was not much bigger (only 49 in 1832).[5] The economy was based on trade in cattle and other agricultural products. The most important links were with England, especially Liverpool and Whitehaven, and the Isle of Man. There was also trade with Ireland. Modern transport links have meant that the Irish connection is that which is remembered while that with England is often forgotten. The Irish connection 'gave rise to unique social tension through immigration, whereas the links with England and the Isle of Man led to emigration and trade'.[6]

FIGURE 2
An example of a wide house in George Street. Although it appears older than its neighbours, this example seems to share gables with them, and its only chimney is of brick. Note also the different ways of defining the wall edges (quoins defined with paint on the left, and a painted pilaster to the right), and the different chimney types (Paula Martin)

FIGURE 3
Three examples of reused stonework. Top, an architectural stone used on top of a later gate pier; centre, two roll-moulded stones rebuilt into the back and pend walls of the post office; bottom, a chimney incorporating reused and carved stones
(all by Richard Oram)

The windmill which once stood at the southern end of the town was for many years the most visible building, though from some directions the present tolbooth tower does stand out. The priory church may have had a tall tower which would have been visible from the sea, as at other pilgrimage sites, but pilgrims generally approached from the chapel at Isle of Whithorn and a way-marked route would have led them towards their first sight of the priory.

Executive summary

➢ Whithorn developed around the original monastic community, which itself grew up around the supposed burial place of St Ninian.
➢ Whithorn became a burgh of barony c 1312, and was never formally created a royal burgh.
➢ Whithorn was a major pilgrimage site, but royal patronage was on a lesser scale than at other sites such as Tain.
➢ The town's fortunes declined after the Reformation, and it became simply a small market town for its agricultural hinterland.
➢ The footprint of the town expanded markedly between c 1750 and 1832.
➢ Post-Reformation Whithorn flourished most in the late eighteenth and early nineteenth century, and then between c 1840 and c 1880, based on maritime trade through Isle of Whithorn.

Timeline

c 150	Reference to a settlement at *Leukophibia* in the *Geography* of the Alexandrian writer Ptolemy, believed to refer to Whithorn
c 450	Latinus Stone erected
c 450–500	'Ninianic' monastery established at Whithorn
c 640–70	Northumbrian takeover of Galloway
c 700	Northumbrian monastery established
c 730	Creation of a bishopric at Whithorn by the Northumbrians. Pechthelm first named bishop
c 836–40	Last known Northumbrian bishop, Heathured, at Whithorn
c 950–1000	Hiberno-Norse settlement in Galloway
1014	According to late saga tradition, the Icelander Kari Solmundarson and his men over-winter at Whithorn in the house of Jarl Melkólfr
1128	Revival of see of Whithorn with Gilla-Aldan as first bishop
c 1177	Establishment of Premonstratensian convent [priory] to serve cathedral at Whithorn
1234	Death of Alan, lord of Galloway
1286	Cathedral damaged during raids into Galloway by the Bruce family after the death of King Alexander III
1301	Pilgrimage by Edward, Prince of Wales, to St Ninian's shrine
c 1312	Edward Bruce grants a charter of burgh of barony in favour of the prior of Whithorn
1325	Confirmation charter as burgh of barony, belonging to the priory (original charter probably 1312–15), and first reference to port at Isle of Whithorn
1329	Pilgrimage by Robert I
1450	Confirmation charter by James II, with prior given regality, and more privileges to burgesses
1459	Another confirmation charter
1473	Pilgrimage by Margaret of Denmark
1488–1508	Pilgrimages by James IV
1511	Another confirmation charter, clarifying rights to international trade (ambiguous enough to allow the town to claim royal burgh status)
1531	Whithorn first appears in stent roll of royal burghs
1563	Visit of Mary, Queen of Scots, to Whithorn
1574	Whithorn first sends representatives to the Convention of Royal Burghs
1581	Pilgrimage banned
c 1610	Former priory church becomes cathedral for new Protestant diocese of Galloway

1641	Whithorn first sends a representative to parliament
1661	Confirmation charter
1709	Tolbooth rebuilt
c 1790	Pier built at the Isle
1793	Secession Church built, St John Street
1814	New town hall and prison
1822	New parish church
1844	Free Church built at Isle of Whithorn
1852	Gas works opened
1860–65	Whithorn Academy built
1877	Arrival of railway
1882	Iron Roman Catholic church built
1885–86	New town hall, St John Street, opened
1892	United Presbyterian (formerly Secession) church, St John Street, rebuilt
1898	Extension to new town hall
c 1900	Belmont Hall built for Good Templars
1902	Whithorn creamery opened
1911	Public Library, St John Street, opened
1924	First modern Roman Catholic pilgrimage
1935	First council housing in Wigtownshire, including at Isle
1935	Electricity and mains water supply
1950	Last passenger train
1959–60	Roman Catholic church built
1964	Last goods train

Notes

1   For a general history of pilgrimage in Scotland, see P Yeoman, *Pilgrimage in Medieval Scotland* (London, 1999)

2   The longest rigs, behind the houses at the southern end of the east side of George Street, seem to have been lengthened after *c* 1750 (traces of the earlier boundary wall can still be seen on the 1849 OS map)

3   This feature was removed when the rigs were truncated to create the cemetery extension (see **fig 15**)

4   *Report on Municipal Corporations in Scotland* (1835), 429. The parliamentary boundary had recently been extended, I MacLeod, *Discovering Galloway* (Edinburgh, 1986), 224

5   *Report on Municipal Corporations*, 429

6   R H Campbell, *Owners and Occupiers: Changes in Rural Society in South-West Scotland before 1914* (Aberdeen, 1991), 6

2: *Site and setting*

The climate of Galloway is mild in the winter, but relatively cool in summer. This, combined with the effects of glaciation, produces potential arable land only under about 500 feet (152m), meaning that much of the land is better suited to pastoral farming.[1] Mild winters allow cattle to remain outside, saving the cost of both buildings and fodder.

Galloway has a long coastline, but the large tidal range, combined with silting, made the harbours east of Garlieston increasingly hard to access. As the size and draught of ships increased, and steam replaced sail, these ports, including Isle of Whithorn, gradually fell out of use. Stranraer was the main survivor. In addition, the railways gradually replaced coastal shipping, while long-distance travel routes changed, first with the advent of steam shipping, then with railways. More recently, dual carriageways and car-

FIGURE 4
Air photograph of Whithorn, looking south towards Isle of Whithorn (Crown copyright: RCAHMS)

FIGURE 5
Air photograph of Isle
of Whithorn, looking
north (Crown copyright:
RCAHMS)

ferries have become the preferred means of travel, and Whithorn now lies further from major travel routes than it did in the past, both physically and psychologically.

The burgh of Whithorn stands at the centre of the parish of the same name (**fig 4**), which extends to *c* 10,000 acres (4047 ha). 'The face of the country is variegated with hills and valleys. In some places, the land is broken, and appears barren at a distance, but upon examination, it is found deep and rich. Such land here is dry, provided with shelter, and of the first quality for grazing. The soil of this parish is in general fertile, divided by stone walls, covered with lime, sea shells or marl, and produces rich crops, or feeds the best cattle'.[2] 'In point of scenery, this parish has nothing to boast of; the surface is almost level, and has neither mountain nor glen, hill nor dale, wood nor forest, to interrupt its uniformity'.[3]

Situated two miles (3.2km) inland, and 220 feet (67m) above sea level, Whithorn is 10 miles from Wigtown, 20 from Newton Stewart, and 32 from Stranraer (16km, 32km, and 51.5km respectively). Isle of Whithorn, two and a half miles (4km) to the south-east, is Whithorn's outport, and the most southerly village in Scotland (**fig 5**) (**maps 1 & 2**).

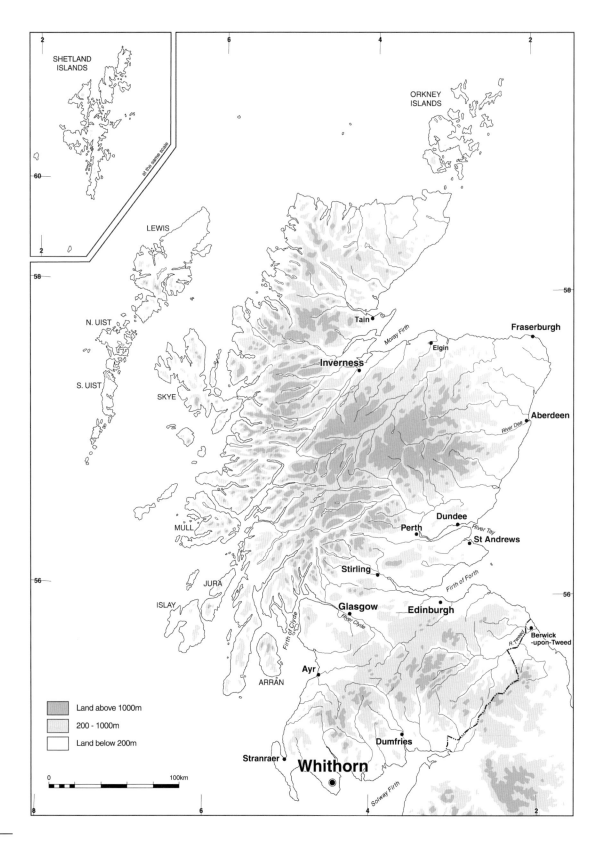

ORKNEY
ISLANDS

at the same scale

LEWIS

N. UIST

S. UIST

SKYE

MULL

JURA

ISLAY

ARRAN

Tain

Moray Firth

Elgin

Fraserburgh

Inverness

Aberdeen

River Dee

Dundee

Perth

River Tay

St Andrews

Stirling

Firth of Forth

Glasgow

Edinburgh

River Clyde

Firth of Clyde

Berwick
-upon-Tweed

R. Tweed

Ayr

Dumfries

Stranraer

Whithorn

Solway Firth

Land above 1000m

200 - 1000m

Land below 200m

0   100km

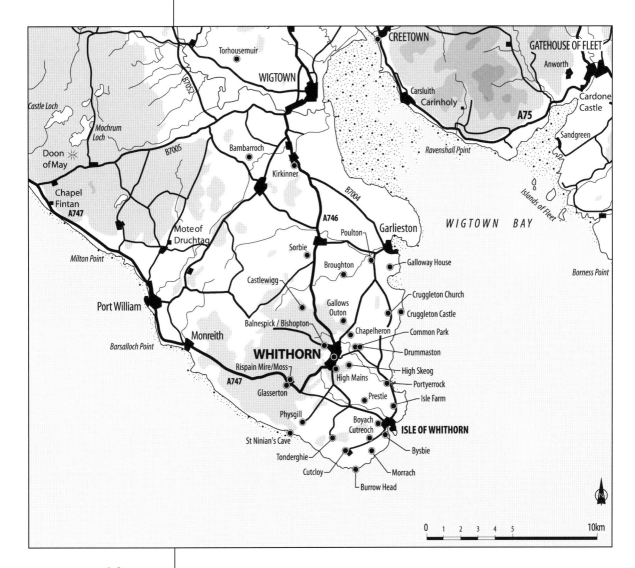

MAP 1 (left)
Location map

MAP 2
Whithorn and the southern
Machars

Building materials and details

The most common rock in the parish is greywacke, a type of hard, brittle sandstone that breaks into thin horizontal strips; it is almost impossible to carve. The dominant facing material in Whithorn today, it has been used in two ways. Stones in older fabric are thinner, greyer and less sharp-edged, whereas nineteenth-century facing greywacke is slightly thicker, sharp-cut, grey-green in colour and heavily streaked with orange-brown iron (**fig 6**). There is also a considerable tradition of drystone walling for garden, rig and boundary walls (**fig 7**).

Marble and slate were available from nearby Burrow Head, but were not extensively used.[4] Some entire earlier portions of the priory, along with the finer details, were built with silver and red sandstone, both of which appear to have come from the Dundrennan area.[5] The thirteenth-century nave was built of greywacke, which suggests that it was probably harled. In the mid-nineteenth century it was noted that 'There are no continued beds of granite, but large detached blocks are met with here and there'. Large pieces of rough granite, of unknown origin, were used for lintels, dressings and quoins toward the end of the nineteenth century.[6] Most seventeenth-century gravestones are of greywacke, but the majority of eighteenth- and nineteenth-century ones are of imported sandstone. By the end of the nineteenth century granite was the stone of choice.[7]

'A great part of the present town seems to have been built chiefly from the ruins of the priory. There are few of the old houses without some of the freestone in their walls'.[8] A century later this is still true. Robbed sandstone details from the priory abound throughout the town. In particular, it was customary to use crisply cut greywacke with red sandstone margins in the later nineteenth century refronting of houses on George Street, of which an excellent example is no. 87, home of the architect and archaeologist William Galloway (**fig 6**). In many instances, the edges of those margins reveal that they are reused stones, presumably from the priory. At the time of such refronting, the chimney-stacks were panelled in red ashlar. The only semi-complete feature of a pre-eighteenth-century Whithorn house, apart from the archway into the priory, is the doorway of no. 5 George Street which retains most of its roll-moulding, with an abraded trace of a keel moulding (**fig 8**).

There is the occasional use of white-yellow brick in nineteenth-century rear extensions to some of the houses (**fig 9**), or as smart dressings for extensions and halls. Red and blue-glazed brick – and indeed English architecture – makes its appearance at Oswie Villa (**fig 10**), built by James Duff, grain-merchant and ship-owner from Isle of Whithorn (1830–86), near the station, perhaps symbolic of the move from shipping to railway transport.

FIGURE 6
An example of the later nineteenth-century use of the local greywacke stone with painted margins: no. 87 George Street, the home of William Galloway, architect and archaeologist
(Paula Martin)

FIGURE 7
The boundary wall at the end of the rigs at the south-western end of the town
(Richard Oram)

FIGURE 8 (above)
Old doorway with roll
mouldings (typically pre-
1650) at no. 5 George Street
(Richard Oram)

FIGURE 9 (top right)
An example of the decorative
use of yellow brick on the
back of a house on the east
side of George Street
(Paula Martin)

FIGURE 10 (right)
Oswie Villa, built by a
local merchant in brick in
an English style, near the
railway station
(Paula Martin)

There is surprisingly little harling in Whithorn, although there is evidence that it was once more common. Instead, the more recent preference appears to be for the English pattern of either exposed stonework, or many coats of gloss paint, whose relative thinness increases the apparent size and scale of the stone margins. There is more genuine colour in the exposed mid-nineteenth-century greywacke and its lurid window margins. A detail particular to the town is a shiny, rusticated edge-pilaster, usually painted,

FIGURE 11
No. 29 George Street, with
a fanlight and a heavy
cornice, but otherwise
the typical Whithorn
exposed greywacke,
with painted margins to
doors, windows, walls and
chimneys (Richard Oram)

FIGURE 12
No. 79 George Street, with
doorpiece added to create a
separate entrance when the
building was converted for
use as a bank in the 1840s
(Paula Martin)

often in red, signalling the edge of a given property, but promiscuously used over more than one separate building, or perhaps even used on its own (**figs 1, 2 & 13**). Other than a number of fanlights, notably at no. 29 George Street (**fig 11**), the black-columned porch of the former bank at no. 79 (**fig 12**), and the curious Grecian cornices and shallow pediment above a three-doored

FIGURE 13

No. 48 St John Street, with
cornices and a pediment over
the ground-floor opening,
and painted pilasters flanking
the door. As the window
and door surround have not
been painted a contrasting
colour, the pilasters flanking
the door have had their fill
coloured (Richard Oram)

centrepiece at no. 48 St John Street (**fig 13**), typical Scots details in terms of cornices, skews, skewputts, or pilasters are few – and generally English in derivation.

It seems clear from thackstanes that most roofs were once thatched, and even by the 1790s not all of them had yet been re-covered in slate.[9] However, the three-dimensional Scots slate and Scottish roofing techniques are relatively infrequent, and the roofing details appear much more English/Irish. More common are the thinner, squarer English slates, and English ridge details (or lack of them). Indeed, at roof-level, it would be difficult to distinguish most Whithorn buildings from those of northern England. A considerable number of roofs are covered in felt, corrugated iron or corrugated asbestos. A small number of pantiles survive on derelict outhouses. There is a certain amount of decorative detail, but it is slight. No. 107 George Street has a pleasant cast-iron gutter, and there are a few brackets and octagonal chimney pots.

Street-names

Most street-names were changed at some date between the 1st edition OS map (1849; **map 8**) and the 2nd edition (1894; **map 9**). Main Street became George Street; East Port (or Low Port, or Paldrite Street[10]) became St John Street; West Port (earlier High Port) became High Street; Back Row became Green Lane; The Row (formerly Rotten, then Routine, Row) became Free Church Row, and then King's Road.[11] At least some of these name changes seem to have been antiquarian in intent. Bruce Street commemorates the pilgrimage by Robert I in 1329; St John Street the possession of property in Whithorn by the Knights of St John; Castle Hill the supposed castle site; and Oswie Villa a reference to Oswiu, king of Northumbria, who was believed to have stayed in Whithorn. Only George Street so far eludes identification. The northern narrowing was called Port Mouth, and the southern one Isle Port Mouth.[12]

Notes

1   I Morrison, 'Galloway: Locality and Landscape Evolution', in R D Oram and G P Stell (eds), *Galloway: Land and Lordship* (Edinburgh, 1991), 13–14

2   *OSA*, 535–6

3   *NSA*, 54

4   *OSA*, 540–1

5   We would like to thank Ray Chadburn for giving us sight of the final draft of his article 'Building stone sources for Whithorn Priory, Dundrennan Abbey and other Historic Buildings in Galloway', *TDGNHAS* lxxxi (2007), 63–9, which discusses the quarries in Kirkbean and Rerrick parishes, including the Walls Hill site which appears to be the source of some of the sandstone employed at Whithorn

6   *NSA*, 53. It has been suggested that some of the granite seen in local buildings derives from such erratic boulders

7   J E Birchman, Old Kirkyard, Whithorn, typescript list of monumental inscriptions, nd (courtesy of John Pickin, Stranraer Museum), 1

8   P H M'Kerlie, *History of the Lands and their Owners in Galloway*, 2 vols (Edinburgh, 1870, reprinted, ed Gardner, Paisley, 1906), 417–84

9   *OSA*, 533

10   G Fraser, *Lowland Lore; or the Wigtownshire of long ago* (Wigtown, 1880), 114; there is local memory of the name Poldricht associated with the area near the library

11   Local oral testimony is that once it became a footpath it was called 'Queen's Way'

12   These names are in current use but not on maps

3: *Archaeology and history*

Prehistory

A range of finds recorded by the National Monuments Record of Scotland (NMRS) indicates a human presence from early times. Important palaeoenvironmental evidence has been recovered from Rispain Mire which has the potential to provide information on the early post-glacial landscape of the area.[1] This work has identified human impact on the local vegetation from the Mesolithic onwards.

Stone axes, mace-heads and other stone tools have been recovered from Chapelheron, the old town hall garden, and from unlocated findspots within the parish.[2] Several of these are held in the collections of Stranraer Museum, Glasgow Museums and Art Galleries, and the National Museums of Scotland.[3] Bronze Age cup-and-ring-marked and spiral-marked stones have been identified at Gallows Outon and on the former Golf Course.[4]

Trial excavations in the Manse Field have identified an enclosure ditch which has been radiocarbon dated to the Bronze Age, and a pit containing a thumbnail scraper, suggesting a possible settlement within cultivated land very close to the town.[5] Two bronze axes are recorded as having been recovered from unlocated findspots near the town.[6] Iron Age promontory forts are located at Court Hill, High Skeog and on Isle of Whithorn at Isle Head. The former was identified in 1958 by the presence of a possible enclosure wall which delimited an area *c* 10 x 14m in extent.[7] The latter consists of a multivallate fort and possible remains of a hut circle.[8] A description of this site is included in a survey of promontory forts along the north Solway coastline.[9] The cropmark of a Bronze Age ring-ditch enclosure has also been identified on the Isle,[10] and there are clearance mounds and cultivation furrows between the village and the chapel, although these may be later.[11]

Roman

It is possible that Whithorn is the settlement of *Leukophibia* mentioned in Ptolemy's *Geography* of the mid-second century AD. The name, meaning the shining or white place, is equivalent to the later Latin name, *Candida Casa*.[12] That there was activity in the area at this time is confirmed by the presence of several Roman coins, recorded as stray finds at Chapelheron, and from a garden and other unrecorded locations in Whithorn.[13] These are of second- to third-century date.

Thomas reported that possible Roman cremation burials were found during Ritchie's excavations at the priory site in the 1950s,[14] and a few other objects of Roman date have turned up in the more recent excavations by the Whithorn Trust.[15] These include sherds of several samian and coarseware pottery vessels, fragments of glass vessels, mosaic tesserae, a fourth-century coin, some copper-alloy objects, and possibly a millstone. All of these were found in post-Roman contexts, which has led to some debate concerning their origins; they may represent curated or scavenged objects from an abandoned military site, possibly in the vicinity of Newton Stewart, or occupation of Roman date at Whithorn.

A roadway which formed the earliest phase of activity identified in the Glebe Field excavations may be of late Roman or early post-Roman date.[16] At present, however, the archaeological evidence for this period is tantalisingly limited and not substantial enough to equate Whithorn with any certainty to the important trading and power-centre that *Leukophibia* is likely to have been. It is thus important that any opportunity to investigate known Roman findspots should be taken.

Early Historic and medieval periods

Early Historic archaeology

Whithorn is known to archaeologists throughout Europe as an important Early Christian site. This is due largely to the excavations carried out by the Whithorn Trust in the 1980s and 1990s, but earlier work also provided much valuable information regarding the structure and material culture of the early 'monastery'. Traditionally Whithorn was the site of *Candida Casa,* the white stone church built by St Ninian, a fifth-century British bishop.

Early excavations by William Galloway in the 1880s, Ralegh Radford in 1949–53, P R Ritchie in 1957–67 and Chris Tabraham in 1972 and 1975 have been summarised by Hill.[17] The Whithorn Trust excavations carried out from 1984 to 1991 have been fully published,[18] and there are interim reports on the 1992–96 investigations by the University of Bradford and York Archaeological Trust,[19] and further work by Headland Archaeology Ltd from 2001.[20] The sequence of archaeological deposits is complex and provides evidence for many phases of activity from the sixth century onwards. It is not possible or necessary to repeat these findings in detail here, but a brief summary of the work to date is presented, as the presence of the early monastic community is fundamental to the siting and subsequent development of the burgh.

Most of the excavations prior to those by the Whithorn Trust concentrated on the immediate environs of the medieval priory (see below), within the present Kirk Field and churchyard (**fig 14**). An early stone building was located to the east of the remains of the priory church and was identified as part of the early ecclesiastical centre by Radford, although Hill suggests that

FIGURE 14
Excavations in Whithorn
churchyard in the 1980s
(Crown copyright: Historic
Scotland)

it may belong to the eighth century.[21] These excavations were able to show that medieval levelling of the area around the cathedral nave had removed any traces of the early monastery on the summit of the hill, although early graves survived to the east.

Test-pits by Tabraham in 1972 in the Glebe Field to the south of Bruce Street revealed the presence of complex stratigraphy which was to become the focus for large-scale excavations by Hill in 1984–91. The earliest occupation associated with the early monastery has been tentatively dated to the late fifth or early sixth century. Hill interprets the excavation results as showing evidence for cultivation and construction, together with insubstantial buildings located outwith and to the south-west of the postulated inner precinct enclosure (**fig 15**). By the mid-sixth century the inner precinct had grown to encompass a large part of the excavated area and during the subsequent two centuries it contained three successive phases of 'shrines' and associated graveyards within the precinct, and several phases of workshops outside.

The early eighth century saw the development of the Northumbrian minster recorded by Bede, identified archaeologically by a change in orientation of the 'inner precinct', and new structures interpreted as oratories, a burial enclosure and guest quarters. By the beginning of the ninth century, the oratories had been converted into a wooden church and the burial enclosure had become a mortuary or burial chapel. A period of decline and crisis was experienced in the mid-ninth century: the church became a barn and was subsequently burnt down, the guest quarters were dismantled and reverted to arable land, and the area surrounding the higher ground of the precinct was flooded. Restoration and rebuilding followed rapidly, with a new timber church erected on the same site, reconstruction of the burial chapel and construction of a new settlement on the higher ground away from the floodplain. The new church lasted about a century before it was replaced by a group of smaller

FIGURE 15
Aerial photograph looking west of the area of the Whithorn Priory precinct. The Glebe Field, where excavations revealed evidence for an earlier secular settlement, can be seen to the left of the priory, behind the buildings on the west side of George Street (Crown copyright: RCAHMS)

wattle buildings in the mid-tenth century. Rebuilding of the settlement took place intermittently. By the end of the tenth or beginning of the eleventh century it consisted of densely packed small structures on a new alignment which may have formed an outer ring around a new focus, whether religious or mercantile in nature, to the west. The early eleventh century saw further expansion, made possible by the draining of the flooded areas surrounding the settlement. New buildings were located on the reclaimed land and an open area to the west was enlarged; this appears to have been used as a market-place. In this period the buildings and artefacts suggest Hiberno-Norse influence. The archaeological evidence suggests that settlement continued in this form until the late thirteenth century (see below).

Excavations were carried out in Fey Field to the west of the priory between 1992 and 1996.[22] Again, a complex sequence of paths and structures was revealed, with evidence of activity from the sixth century onwards. Building types were similar to those found in the Glebe Field, the earliest consisting of insubstantial wattle buildings, followed by vertical timbers and planks set in slots in the ground, and the latest being wattle and daub with clay floors. Evidence for ferrous and non-ferrous metalworking was found, as well as a possible aqueduct and water system. The southern part of the field contained a graveyard which probably dated from the sixth to seventh centuries originally, but continued in use through several phases, interspersed by levelling layers. Geophysical survey over the south-eastern corner of the field showed that further stone buildings await investigation. Evidence that the graveyard continued slightly further to the south-east was recovered during a watching brief to monitor the replacement of telegraph poles in 1998–99, when human remains were recovered adjacent to the boundary wall with Bruce Street.[23] A watching brief along the line of an electricity cable included four small trenches to the west of the Manse, but these (along with four other trenches excavated further to the south as part of the project) revealed nothing of archaeological interest.[24]

Hill identified several possible precinct boundaries at various phases on the Glebe Field site, but the evidence was based on short lengths of ditches or more ephemeral remains.[25] These were extrapolated to suggest oval inner and outer zones. He also suggested a larger enclosure which may have encompassed the lands of the monastery. This evidence was assessed by Lowe,[26] who found that the outermost boundary forming the larger enclosure was 'largely an artefact of topography' and suggested a new boundary enclosing some 7.5 ha around and to the west of the monastic site. He suggested further fieldwork to determine the validity of this hypothesis. Subsequent evaluation trenches did not identify any physical boundaries in the expected locations, but found an area of light-industrial and agricultural activity in the eastern half of the Manse Field.[27] Further trial excavations in this area revealed a possible sunken-featured building of the late first millennium AD.[28] Evaluation trenches in the fields to the west were largely negative in terms of archaeological features, although a few ditches were recorded. The monastic settlement appears on current evidence to be contained within the fields immediately adjacent to the priory site, concentrated largely to the south and west.

The Whithorn Museum holds a large collection of stonework, including cross-shafts and headstones of the 'Whithorn School' and other carved stones dating from the mid-fifth to the twelfth century.[29] These include the 'Latinus' stone, an inscribed slab discovered during Galloway's late nineteenth-century excavations at the priory, and the 'Peter' stone, probably originally located by the road to Isle of Whithorn and perhaps marking the boundary of the monastic lands (**fig 16**). Further examples are held by the National Museums of Scotland. A tenth- or eleventh-century cross-slab was recovered more recently during the demolition of a wall at no. 62 George Street in 1992, where it had been reused as a door lintel (**fig 17**). Stonework of this type is very likely to have been built into the fabric of other structures within the town.

The majority of these stones and crosses would have stood at significant places within the ecclesiastical site at Whithorn. They protected boundaries, churches and the Christian dead. The crosses of the Whithorn School were created in a workshop on site between the later tenth and early twelfth century. The large scale of production indicates the importance of the place as a centre of ecclesiastical power.

Although it is now considered unlikely that Isle of Whithorn was the site of the original foundation by St Ninian (see below), there is little doubt that from

FIGURE 16
The Peter stone, a cross and the Latinus stone; height of cross 1.63m
(Crown copyright: Historic Scotland)

FIGURE 17
Conservation work in progress on the recently discovered Packard Stone
(Crown copyright: Historic Scotland)

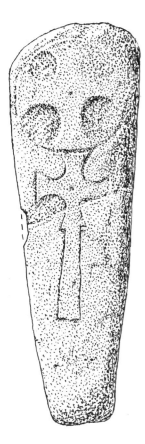

FIGURE 18
Early Christian cross-slab
from St Ninian's Cave;
height 0.66m (WHP.C3)
(Crown copyright: Historic
Scotland)

earliest times Whithorn relied heavily on the port for trade and provisions, imported goods, and visiting pilgrims. Place-name evidence suggests that a farm belonging to the bishop was located on the mainland near the harbour in the ninth or tenth century.[30] Hill suggests that the most likely early route between the town and the Isle was the path which now enters Whithorn via King's Road.[31] It is more likely, however, that this was a pedestrian pilgrim route as distinct from a road, possibly on the same alignment as the present one, suitable for ox-carts to transport heavy loads such as wine from the port to the priory.

In the nearby parish of Glasserton, at the west end of Physgill Bay, the feature known as St Ninian's Cave[32] would have been a calling point for pilgrims approaching by sea. Seven Early Christian crosses were cut into the rockface outside, suggesting the cave may have been used by Christian recluses (**fig 18**).[33]

Medieval archaeology

Historically, the change from 'Early Historic' to 'medieval' is marked by the foundation of the Premonstratensian priory/convent in the twelfth century. The archaeological evidence for the priory is based on work carried out by Radford and others (see above), and interpreted by Hill in conjunction with his own work. While the foundation of the new cathedral clearly involved major building works, these appear to have had little effect on the daily lives of Whithorn's inhabitants. The archaeological record in the Glebe Field exhibits a clear continuity of settlement location, form and type from the eleventh to the late thirteenth century, although by the turn of the thirteenth century the large open space to the west had been encroached upon by housing. The main change was probably an increased involvement in the manufacture and trade of goods, particularly leather- and antler-working. There is little evidence for the form of the twelfth-century cathedral, although it is thought to have been a simple cruciform structure with a short nave. Extension of both choir and nave took place in the following century, and by the end of the thirteenth century a large cemetery had been established in the northern part of the Glebe Field, spreading as far east as the Museum Garden.

A few houses to the south suggest that the remains of the settlement clung on to the outer precinct for a while, but the foundation of the present town in the early fourteenth century provided new opportunities which must have been attractive to the residual population. As the town grew, so did the priory, adding claustral buildings to the north-west and transepts to the east end of the cathedral. The southern graveyard was abandoned by the mid-fifteenth century, moving to a new position which is currently unknown, and the west end of the cathedral was also remodelled at this time, leaving the remains of workshops and construction debris to be discovered in the Glebe Field. Following the closure of the southern graveyard, a large stone building was erected in the Glebe Field in the early sixteenth century. This has been interpreted as the commendator's house. A chapel and large crypts were added to the east end of the cathedral at around the same period.

The boundary wall between the Glebe Field and the rear of the properties along George Street was examined during a watching brief in 1998. This showed that at a depth of 1.2m the boundary wall projected out by 5cm and continued downwards for 'at least five, better laid, courses', although it could not be determined whether this represented an earlier wall.[34] Finds collected during the watching brief indicated that the rear of the property had been used as a rubbish dump in the post-medieval period.

An inventory of 260 pieces of carved stone located at the priory was carried out in 2003–04.[35] The fragments were largely of twelfth- to fifteenth/sixteenth-century date. Very few carved stones survive *in situ* so it was difficult to suggest the original siting of most pieces, but a few were identified as columns from a transept or choir aisle and from the cloister, and there were several fragments of window mullions and flowing tracery. Remote-sensing surveys carried out in 2002 at the east end of the priory identified what may be the south wall of the choir and a stairway down into the crypt, but failed to correlate sub-surface anomalies with grave features suggested by the presence of *in situ* headstones.[36]

Remains associated with the twelfth-century priory were uncovered in the field to the west of the site; these consisted of a covered drain and two stone plinths.[37] A later drain was identified as the main drain of the priory, and there were quarry-pits and middens of probable early fifteenth-century date. Overlying the infilled quarries were the stone foundations of a building interpreted as a byre or stable. To the south were small wicker-and-daub buildings which were contemporary with the cathedral.[38] Medieval burials in the southern part of the field continued on the site of an earlier graveyard.[39] A building similar in size and construction technique to the commendator's house was identified in trial excavations on the Manse Field,[40] and a stone-built, clay-lined conduit was possibly of a similar date. The excavations also revealed several medieval or later linear features.

The layout of the medieval burgh, which documentary evidence suggests was founded between 1312 and 1315 (see below), still survives in the form of burgage plots of varying length and width, which extend behind the eighteenth- and nineteenth-century houses lining George Street. Some of these facades may hide earlier structural remains. The original late medieval gatehouse to the priory (**fig 19**), for example, was significantly altered in the post-medieval period to become no. 53 George Street.[41] Occasional archaeological work within the burgh itself has so far only revealed remains of post-medieval or uncertain date. Castle Hill at the north-east end of the town was claimed by M'Kerlie to be the site of the castle of the Bishops of Galloway, but no trace of this survives above ground.[42]

FIGURE 19
a) The entrance to the priory from George Street (Paula
Martin); b) detail of the royal arms of James IV after paint
conservation by Historic Scotland
(Crown copyright: Historic Scotland)

St Ninian's Chapel on Isle of Whithorn was traditionally regarded as
the site of Ninian's *Candida Casa*, although the identification was already
under question in the later nineteenth century.[43] The current roofless
structure is dated to only *c* 1300, with nineteenth-century rebuilding (**fig 20**).
Radford's excavations identified an earlier structure of twelfth- or early
thirteenth-century date, but yielded no evidence for a fifth- to twelfth-century
ecclesiastical presence on the site. Part of the original enclosure survives as
turf-covered footings.

FIGURE 20
Drawing by General Pitt-
Rivers of the chapel at Isle of
Whithorn (Crown copyright:
Historic Scotland)

CHAPEL OF THE ISLE,
ISLE OF WHITHORN, WIGTONSHIRE.
VIEW LOOKING S.W. (OCT. 1887)

Early Historic and medieval history

Disentangling myth from history in the Early Historic period at Whithorn has been the subject of much scholarly endeavour since the nineteenth century but especially in the second half of the twentieth century. Much of this research has been focused on the dating of the 'Ninianic' mission and the development of the first Christian community at the site. All the surviving documentary evidence relating to this first phase, however, is of eighth-century composition and appears to be a largely propagandist development to suit the claims of the Northumbrian church over the Columban tradition based on Iona. Little that is concrete can be said, other than that the area around Whithorn may have lain within the Brittonic kingdom known as Rheged, but even this cannot be established with confidence.

In the seventh century the Brittonic kingdom of Rheged and the region that we know as Galloway was absorbed into the expanding Northumbrian kingdom. This development is usually presented as a consequence of the marriage of the future Northumbrian king, Oswiu, to the heiress of Rheged, Riemmelth, but there is debate as to whether this was achieved peacefully or violently.[44] Union or conquest in the mid-seventh century was followed by an influx of Northumbrian colonists, whose presence is attested by the liberal scattering of Anglian settlement-names throughout the region.[45] One of the main concentrations appears to have been in the southern Machars, where the place-name Whithorn itself is of Anglian derivation (*hwit-aern* = the white steading or shack). Whithorn appears to have emerged as one of the principal centres of Northumbrian political power in the region, a status reinforced by the establishment there in *c*730 of a diocesan centre.[46] Historical evidence relating to the development of this Northumbrian religious community is very limited, comprising principally a list of bishops and some incidental detail relating to the character of the monastic establishment fossilised within a Latin *Life* of St Ninian. The archaeological evidence, however, points to the evolution of a substantial complex positioned at the heart of a landed estate whose economy was geared towards the support of the monastery.[47]

After the collapse of the Northumbrian kingdom in the mid-ninth century, Whithorn again lapses into historical obscurity, although the archaeological record reveals continuity of activity on the site. In the early 900s, the northern shores of the Solway appear to have been receiving a significant influx of Scandinavian settlers, associated mainly with Norse settlement in Ireland and the Hebrides, and place-names reveal a significant concentration of such settlement in the Machars peninsula around Whithorn.[48] The Norse presence at Whithorn, although drawing Galloway more generally into an Irish Sea network, may have served to preserve the links with York which had been forged during the Northumbrian period. Certainly, in the later ninth and tenth centuries, Whithorn was part of a cultural and political world which spanned the Irish Sea and stretched from York to Dublin. It is likely, given the maintenance of the York connection, that one important focus on the site continued to be religious, and it has been suggested that the succession of bishops may in fact have continued through the documentary 'Dark Age'.[49]

The only possible reference to Whithorn between the early ninth and early twelfth century, however, is a mention in *Njal's Saga*, a late thirteenth-century Icelandic composition which deals with ostensibly early eleventh-century events. This saga mentions that in 1014 a party of Icelanders overwintered in Scotland at a place called *Hvitsborg* in the house of a Jarl Melkólfr.[50] There has been considerable speculation as to the specific location and nature of the jarl's residence, but it seems most likely that it was at Whithorn.[51] Given the late date at which the saga was composed, however, there are dangers inherent in using it to argue for the existence at Whithorn of a high-status Gaelic-Scandinavian secular settlement. But when taken in conjunction with the archaeological evidence, there emerges a strong possibility that the earlier ecclesiastical focus may have been laicised and redeveloped as a secular political and economic centre during the tenth century. It is impossible on the basis of the available evidence, however, to be more categorical.

Through the eleventh century, parts of Galloway appear to have formed an element within a kingdom built upon sea-power which at times embraced Dublin and Man, and possibly the southern Hebrides. Western Galloway's cultural orientation appears to have been principally westward-looking, perhaps reflecting a closer integration into the hybrid world of the Norse-Gaelic sea-kingdoms of the Irish Sea and Hebrides than into the remainder of mainland Scotland.[52] Again, however, the evidence for this connection is physical and archaeological rather than documentary, and attempts to construct an elaborate history for western Galloway generally, and Whithorn specifically, as the seat of a Norse-Gaelic or Gall-Gaidhil lordship must be viewed with great caution.

Whithorn only re-emerges fully into the historical record in the early twelfth century when it was established as the seat of a revived episcopal see. This revival may have been based on a community of secular priests and clerks who had perhaps continued to serve a church on the site through the undocumented ninth to early twelfth century. In December 1128 Pope Honorius II instructed an unnamed bishop-elect of Whithorn to present himself to his 'appropriate metropolitan', Archbishop Thurstan of York, for consecration.[53] Shortly afterwards, one Gilla-Aldan, bishop of Whithorn, gave his oath of obedience to Thurstan.[54] This revival of an independent bishopric at Whithorn was a significant event linked to the crystallisation of new political alignments in northern Britain and especially in the northern Irish Sea and Southern Upland region of Scotland. It appears to have been a manifestation of the emergence of a new power in this zone, the kingdom or lordship of Galloway, ruled until 1160 by Fergus, founder of one of the most powerful dynasties in twelfth- and early thirteenth-century

Britain.[55] Gilla-Aldan was possibly Fergus's appointee, perhaps being linked with the minster at Kirkcudbright, which appears to have been the original power-base of Fergus's family in eastern Galloway.[56] Gilla-Aldan swore obedience to the Archbishop of York at a time when David I of Scotland was seeking to end any question of Scottish bishops accepting the spiritual overlordship of an English archbishop. This indicates both the strength of the traditional links between Whithorn and the old Northumbrian church, and the independent political stance taken by Galloway's rulers, who cultivated close ties with the English crown. In the twelfth and thirteenth centuries, the Whithorn-York tie had been a key factor in forming Galloway's distinct cultural and spiritual character, and in preserving its strongly independent identity in the face of expanding Scottish influence. The south- and eastward perspectives of Galloway were to remain a dominant element in shaping regional development throughout the Middle Ages and beyond. Whithorn remained a suffragan diocese of York into the fourteenth century, when the strains of war and schism produced a rift. This rift was finally formalised in 1472, with the formal inclusion of Galloway in the new Scottish archdiocese of St Andrews.

Fergus appears to have expanded his power beyond eastern Galloway and constructed his domain in stages from a number of smaller territories. The River Cree (Gaelic, *crithe*, a boundary, division) appears to have formed a major early frontier within the region. Westwards lay part of the former kingdom of the Rhinns, whose rulers in the eleventh century had intermittently controlled possessions stretching from Dublin and Man to the southern Hebrides.[57] This district, the later thirteenth-century sheriffdom of Wigtown, became one of the principal components of Fergus's domain. Cruggleton Castle, on the sea-cliffs east of Whithorn, formed one of his chief seats of power.[58] The juxtaposition of the castle of the lords of Galloway and the cathedral of the diocese symbolised the pairing of the two main authorities in the region. The closeness of the relationship between the two was perhaps also indicated by the architectural similarities between the twelfth-century church at Cruggleton and the Romanesque details of the earliest twelfth-century work at Whithorn, suggesting that the same masons worked on both structures.[59] Fergus, too, is credited with the original foundation of a priory of regular canons attached to the cathedral at Whithorn. This development not only aided the bishop in his work of spiritual reform and ecclesiastical reorganisation in his diocese, but also provided Fergus and his heirs with a locally influential dependency.[60] The lords of Galloway exercised considerable influence over the bishops, and were instrumental in securing the election of some. Bishop Walter (1209–35), for example, was a former chamberlain of the last and greatest of the male line of lords descended from Fergus, Alan of Galloway. Alan's heirs claimed the right to nominate to the see down to the end of the thirteenth century.[61] The close identification of the political power of the lords of Galloway with the spiritual power of the bishops, and also the local influence of the monastery at Whithorn, ensured that both bishop and prior were key figures in the struggles for control of Galloway after Alan's death. This importance did not necessarily always bode well for Whithorn itself.

Alan's death in 1234 without a legitimate male heir plunged Galloway into crisis.[62] For the preceding half-century, Galloway had been drawn progressively into a closer Scottish orbit. Scotland's aggressively expansionist king, Alexander II, was determined to complete the process of integration presented to him by this failure of the male line of lords. The result was the enforced partitioning of the lordship between Alan's three legitimate daughters and their mainly English husbands. This ran counter to the wishes of the men of Galloway, who favoured either the passing of the entire inheritance to one of the collateral male lines or to Alan's illegitimate son, Thomas, or Alexander himself assuming the direct lordship.[63] Alexander's rejection of these options triggered a rebellion in 1235 in support of Thomas, which was bloodily suppressed and a supervisory regime imposed on the conquered lordship. This included tight support of the major institutions of the Church in Galloway, which had been closely associated with the native lords and which may have been heavily involved in advancing Thomas's cause. A key component in Scottish political domination of Galloway was the appointment of a Scottish bishop to succeed Bishop Walter in 1235. This process revealed the bitter hostility of the local political and religious leadership, headed by the prior and canons of Whithorn, towards King Alexander, but also their ultimate powerlessness in the face of superior Scottish military and political force.[64]

The Scottish takeover in Galloway probably had significant consequences for the trading community which excavation has revealed had developed around the monastic complex between the later tenth and the twelfth century. As part of the new political settlement of the former lordship, the king of Scots formally granted royal burgh status to the existing communities at Kirkcudbright east of the River Cree and Wigtown to its west, probably at around the same time as a sheriffdom was created at Wigtown. The legal and commercial privileges enjoyed by this new royal burgh are unknown, all Wigtown's early charters having been destroyed, but it is likely that they gave it the same kind of regional trading monopoly and jurisdictional powers as were enjoyed by other Scottish royal burghs of the time. Consequently, the ability of merchants and craftsmen based at Whithorn to traffic and trade would have been significantly diminished, possibly reducing the income of the priory upon which the townsfolk would have been legally dependent. This mid-thirteenth-century formalisation of commercial activity in western Galloway significantly disadvantaged Whithorn and it is likely that successive priors attempted to secure a more privileged status for their own tenants.

Scottish power in Galloway was strengthened progressively through the thirteenth century, with the kings of Scots continuing to appoint their own candidates as bishops of Whithorn. Both bishopric and priory at Whithorn were major elements in the political and landowning regime in the lordship, and influence over these key institutions was vital for achieving regional political domination. This centrality was demonstrated graphically in 1286 when the cathedral-priory appears to have been a target in the raids mounted from Carrick and Annandale into Galloway by the Bruce family against the centres of power of their Balliol and Comyn rivals. The Balliols and Comyns had been major beneficiaries of the redistribution of power in Galloway that had occurred in the decades after 1234, and by 1286 controlled the bulk of the former lordship between them, as well as exercising great influence over the provincial church. On the death of King Alexander III in March 1286, the Bruces had attempted to make a bid for power in the kingless kingdom by striking at the power-bases of their main rivals in the south-west.[65] The seizure of the Balliol stronghold at Buittle in eastern Galloway and the royal castles at Wigtown and Dumfries may have been accompanied by more general actions which targeted the chief political institutions in the region and caused widespread damage to key structures and to the rural economy.[66] Whithorn may have been one of these targets, for in September 1286 Archbishop John le Romeyn of York authorised the issuing of indulgences to those who contributed towards the repair of the cathedral, which had been burned.[67] The indulgence does not mention the cause of the fire, but the dating of the event offers strong circumstantial evidence for it being a consequence of the political disturbances in the region in the spring of 1286.

This possible burning of the cathedral during the Bruces' initial efforts to advance their claims to the Scottish throne was one of many indications of the hostility of Galloway towards the Bruce cause for much of the period from 1286 to 1357. Galloway remained a major centre of entrenched support for the Balliol kingship, and both Robert I and David II struggled to consolidate their authority within the region. The patronage of the church of Whithorn by Edward Bruce, King Robert's younger brother, in the years between c 1310 and 1318, and by Robert himself in the years down to his death in 1329 (see below), should probably be regarded as efforts to curry favour with what was still a highly influential regional institution. A remote and insecure monarchy set the circumstances for the development of a privileged commercial community at the gates of the cathedral-priory.

The cathedral-priory

As discussed above, the monastic community at Whithorn provided the nucleus around which a civil and probably primarily craft- and trade-based settlement developed in the earlier medieval period. The continued evolution and expanding territorial power and wealth of the monastery probably

FIGURE 21
The Whithorn crozier.
Made in England *c* 1175,
the gilded and enamelled
copper-alloy crozier may
have originally belonged to
Bishops Christian (1154–86)
or John (1189–1209) but
continued to be used by their
successors until it was placed
in the grave of one of the
fourteenth-century bishops
(© Trustees of the National
Museums of Scotland)

served as a magnet for the development in the tenth and eleventh centuries of the secular settlement which seems to be revealed in the archaeological record. The priory, by the later Middle Ages, was one of the most important landowning institutions in Galloway, with estates and interests spread from southern Kintyre and Carrick to Man and Kirkcudbright.[68] By the mid-sixteenth century, the priory's income still stood at nearly £3000 Scots;[69] although less than a quarter of the income commanded by the greatest monastery in the kingdom, the priory at St Andrews, it was still an impressive figure, placing it in the upper ranks of the monasteries in terms of wealth. Much of this income was drawn through and disposed of at Whithorn itself and, as in the earlier medieval period, the secular settlement would have benefited significantly from the adjoining presence of a cash- and resource-rich patron. For the twelfth and thirteenth centuries, however, it is the institutional development of the cathedral-priory, rather than the secular settlement dependent upon it, which can be traced in the historical record. The institutional success and social prominence of the priory, and the progressive expansion of its landed estate, provide a good indicator of the probable continued development of its attendant civil community through this otherwise undocumented period in its history.

The conversion into a regular convent of canons of the community of priests which may have survived at the church of Whithorn appears to have been undertaken by Bishop Christian, who had succeeded to the vacant see in 1154 (**fig 21**). At first, these priests may have adopted the Augustinian rule, a route followed at most other Scottish communities where older groups of non-regular clergy were being reorganised, but they appear to have become Premonstratensians in 1177.[70] The regularisation of the community probably entailed significant development of the complex of buildings at the heart of the old monastery, and certainly involved the construction of an enclosed cloister to the north of the church of Bishops Gilla-Aldan and Christian. This cloister may have had ranges only on its east and north quarters, following what appears to have been a standard Premonstratensian plan employed at Prémontré itself and visible in Scotland at Dryburgh Abbey.[71]

The surviving visible architectural evidence, together with the scanty physical evidence recovered during Ralegh Radford's excavations around the priory church, suggest that the first twelfth-century church may have had a short nave, comprising around half of the surviving structure, but a more elaborate east end.[72] It was probably completed before *c* 1150. The extension of the nave may have occurred following the adoption of the Augustinian or Premonstratensian rule in the later twelfth century, but one surviving thirteenth-century lancet in the south wall and the bases of two more in the current wall-head on the north side suggest that the major structural redevelopment occurred after 1200 and more probably after *c* 1250. As the nave accommodated the pre-Reformation parish church of Whithorn, it could be suggested that the doubling in size of the structure in the thirteenth century reflected the growth of the secular population in the surrounding parish. Further evidence for a major post-1250 reordering of the precinct around the cathedral-priory, especially on its south side, points towards the clearer definition of an enclosed area within which the main complex of church and conventual buildings was isolated. This may also point to the substantial physical development of the attendant settlement.[73]

The mid-thirteenth-century expansion of the church, and the reorganisation of the precinct, may also have been driven by the increasing number of canons in the monastic community. The growing importance of the shrine of St Ninian may have helped to generate the revenues necessary for such major construction work. During the election dispute of 1235, 22 canons of Whithorn are named in the record of the election of Odo Ydonc.[74] When the unknown number of novices, chaplains and lay servitors attached to the monastic household are added, it becomes a very significant establishment, requiring an extensive complex of domestic and ancillary buildings in addition to the core church and cloister.

The expanded complex suffered what appears to have been significant fire damage in 1286.[75] The Bruces' responsibility for this burning may be indicated by Edward Bruce's generous patronage of the comunity after *c* 1310, and similar favour shown by his brother, King Robert, also in recompense for the damage inflicted on the priory and its interests during the wars unleashed by the Bruce brothers after 1306. For example, provision for the maintenance of the fabric of the church was made by Robert I in 1322 during a visit to Galloway, when he granted the canons the teind of various crown revenues from Wigtownshire plus a teind of income from the churches of the then vacant see of Whithorn.[76] Further repair work was carried out on parts of the building in the mid-fourteenth century when Sir Fergus MacDowall paid to have the 'quere rycht wele tyle' (the choir well roofed with tile/slate) as a thanks-offering for the miraculous aid given by St Ninian in defeating a force of English raiders.[77]

There are suggestions at the start of the fifteenth century that the priory church was perhaps in a poor condition, although the claim of its dilapidated state had been made to the pope by Bishop Elisaeus Adougan, whose relations with the prior and canons do not always seem to have been cordial. On 11 April 1408 Pope Benedict issued a commission to the archdeacon of Galloway to compel the prior and canons to contribute from their income towards rebuilding costs, the wording of which appears to repeat the language used in the bishop's complaint.[78] The edifice, it stated, was 'unsound' (*debilem*), 'mean' (*vilem*) and 'old, more than is fitting for such a church'. The commission stated that the bishop had wished to contribute as much as possible from his own resources, but they were insufficient, while the convent of only twelve canons, with an income in excess of 500 merks, had repeatedly declined to make any contribution towards the costs. The archdeacon was instructed to ascertain what the situation was and, if the bishop's claims proved true, to assign half the priory's revenues to rebuilding work for the next ten years. There is, unfortunately, no record of the archdeacon's findings.

Some building work was undertaken under the patronage of the Black Douglases. In 1424, Margaret Stewart, Countess of Douglas, granted the canons a portion of her lands at Cruggleton to provide the revenue to pay for the construction of a new chapel and to support one of the canons to celebrate in it.[79] It is unknown where this chapel was, but a Chapel of St Mary or Lady Chapel is first recorded in April 1431, when Prior Thomas supplicated the pope for ratification of the annexation of the revenues of the parish of Longcastle for the support of the chapel he had begun to build.[80] This process was completed in January 1433 when Bishop Alexander annexed the parish church of St Nicholas of Longcastle to the priory and assigned its revenues in common to the canons. In return, the canons would celebrate mass in the Lady Chapel 'adjacent to the choir of the priory church'.[81] The chapel over the long vaulted crypt that extends southwards from the south aisle of the choir, dating to *c* 1500, may represent a later development of the earlier fifteenth-century Lady Chapel, but there is no concrete evidence for that identification.[82] Further repairs appear to have been undertaken in the 1460s, perhaps paid for by the indulgences which the pope in 1462 permitted to be sold to pilgrims who visited the shrine on Palm Sunday, Easter Day, the Feast of the Nativity of John the Baptist (Midsummer), Lammas (1 August) and St Ninian's Day (16 September).[83]

During James IV's first visit to the shrine in November 1491, he gave 18s 'to the drink' to the masons working on the building, possibly on the southern chapel mentioned above.[84] Construction or repair work was still in progress in April 1501 and August 1502 when he ordered payments of 14s 'drinksilver' to the masons.[85] Offerings made by James IV give some idea of the liturgical and devotional arrangements within the church in the late medieval period. On 22 April 1501, on his night-time arrival at Whithorn, he made offerings 'at the towme [tomb] and at the reliques'. This suggests that what were believed to have been the saint's remains had been transferred from the tomb in the crypt below the east end to a shrine perhaps housed in the eastern chapel on the upper level. The following day, he again made offerings at the tomb and the relics, but also at the 'hie altar', which lay in the canons' quire, and the 'Rude [rood] altar', which lay in front of the pulpitum at the east end of the nave. This suggests his involvement in a series of acts of devotion and participation in masses offered at the altars.[86] The accounts of his visit with

Queen Margaret in August 1506 are more detailed. He made offerings at the rood altar and high altar in the church, but also at 'the ferter' (feretory). This implies that the saint's remains were on public display in an elaborate shrine, in the 'utir [outer] kyrk' (probably referring to the nave), 'at the reliques', and at the Lady altar.[87]

The order in which these offerings are listed suggests a defined pilgrimage route through the church, starting at the rood altar in the nave, moving through into the chancel and passing on to the feretory housing the saint's remains in the chapel behind the high altar. From there, pilgrims descended into the crypt to the saint's tomb and other relics by the steps to the north of the high altar, returning to the church by the south stair to make an offering at the high altar. Thence they progressed to the Lady Chapel, which was perhaps housed in the structure projecting south from the chancel, before exiting the building. Early sixteenth-century alterations and extensions may have led to the development of a new circulation route. The possible south stairs to the crypt, for which no architectural evidence survives, may have been removed at this date, with pilgrims instead exiting from the crypt through the doorway at the south end of the undercroft beneath the south-eastern chapel.[88] In 1506, however, James apparently returned to the upper church to make offerings at additional altars. During his visit in April 1501 he also made an offering at what the editor of the *Treasurer's Accounts* described as 'the chapel on the hill', which is possibly a misrendering of 'chapel on the Isle', perhaps indicating that at Whithorn, as at Tain, the sacred landscape extended beyond the primary focus at the saint's shrine.[89]

Little by way of documentary record survives for the nature, extent and condition of the conventual buildings attached to the priory at any period. References to 'the Priouris lutar' (lute player) and 'the ald Priour of Quhithirnis clarscha' (clarsachd player)[90] suggest that, in common with other clerics of his rank, the prior was maintaining a separate household, and that his residence was suitable for entertaining even royal guests. It is not known where the pre-Reformation prior's lodging was, but it is likely to have been close to, if not adjoining, the accommodation of the other canons in the dormitory on the first floor of the east range of the cloister, to preserve the notion of communal living. That monastic tradition had, as at other Scottish monasteries, apparently broken down by the early sixteenth century.[91] Reference in 1538 to a theft of money from 'Dene Andro [Stevinsone's] chalmer in the dortor of Quhitherne' (chamber in the dormitory) suggests that the formerly open space of the dormitory had by then been partitioned into a series of private chambers for the canons.[92]

Although this points to a decline in observance of the Premonstratensian communal life, it does not mean that there was a withering away of the community in the last decades before the Reformation. Indeed, it seems that the convent admitted up to nine new recruits during the 1550s, and the names of at least eleven canons are known *c* 1560, which suggests that there was still an active religious life.[93] Within a few years of the Protestant revolution of 1560, however, the old order in Whithorn had all but disintegrated. The commendator, Malcolm Fleming, appears to have attempted to maintain Roman Catholic observance in the priory and conduct public masses, for which he was condemned before the General Assembly of the new Protestant church in December 1560.[94] But his involvement in Counter-Reformation activities, particularly a brief effort to restore Catholicism generally in south-western Scotland in 1563,[95] led ultimately to his condemnation and outlawry in 1568. Probably before then, however, some of the relics which provided the chief spiritual focus of the church and shrine – in particular one of St Ninian's arms – had been removed for safe-keeping to the Continent, where they survived until the late eighteenth century (they appear to have been destroyed during the French Revolution).[96] Six of Malcolm's canons were not so steadfast: although they may have continued to live in the priory buildings and draw on the monastic revenues, they became readers in the new Protestant Church and served those local parishes once controlled by the priory.[97] As their numbers dwindled through the later sixteenth century, less of the remaining priory revenue would have been spent on the upkeep of the residential buildings, and by the time the last canon died in the 1590s the monastery was probably already ruinous.

'The town of Whithorn, which is called Clachan'

While the history of the monastic community at Whithorn can be traced with some confidence back to the late seventh century AD, and its earlier 'Ninianic' origins less certainly for some centuries further, the documented history of the town and burgh begins only in the early fourteenth century. On 20 May 1325, King Robert I issued a general charter to the prior and canons of Whithorn, confirming all their lands and rights, especially gifts made in the comparatively recent past.[98] Among these was one by his younger brother, Edward Bruce, who as Lord of Galloway granted to the priory, 'the town of Whithorn which is called Clachan, which [he] gave to them in free burgh with a weekly market day and annual fair day'. A second gift by Edward was 'the toll of the isle of Port Witerne'. The king's confirmation is often taken as marking the date of Whithorn's first creation as a free burgh of barony, but his charter is simply a confirmation of an earlier award made by his brother. Edward Bruce appears to have been granted the title of Lord of Galloway by 1312 and, despite becoming Earl of Carrick in 1313 and assuming the title of King of Ireland in 1315, continued to exercise authority over the lordship of Galloway down to his death in October 1318.[99] Given Edward's commitment to military operations in Ireland after May 1315, it is most likely that his gifts to Whithorn were made in the period 1312–15, but they could have been made at any time up to autumn 1318.

The description of Whithorn as 'Clachan', from the Gaelic *clachan*, meaning a village or hamlet with a church, a kirk-town,[100] reveals the presence of an already established settlement adjacent to the cathedral-priory, the community identified during the Phase 1 excavations between 1987 and 1991.[101] Where precisely this *clachan* lay in relation to the monastery by the fourteenth century is unknown, but the archaeological evidence points to the ending of secular activity on the site of the earlier settlement sometime between *c* 1250 and 1300 (when the monastic precinct appears to have been redefined on the south side of the cathedral-priory), suggesting perhaps the relocation of the existing civil community to outside the south gate of that new precinct. What Edward Bruce's grant reveals, however, is that there was already a significant lay community dependent on the priory before *c* 1312 and serving the needs of what may already have been substantial pilgrim traffic. Rights to a market and an annual fair, presumably held around the Feast of St Ninian, when the numbers of visitors to the shrine would have been highest,[102] would have brought considerable income to the priory.

In April 1408 Bishop Elisaeus Adougan, who was attempting to secure papal assistance to compel the prior and canons to contribute towards the costs of repairs at the cathedral, claimed that 'people are wont to resort [there] in great multitudes'.[103] The implication must be that the burgh was thriving as a service centre for pilgrims, although the bishop may have been overstating the case, hoping to influence the pope's decision. Indeed, suggestions of pilgrims thronging to the shrine rest awkwardly with the claims made by Bishop Elisaeus and reported in a papal mandate issued to the Provost of Lincluden only one month later.[104] In this document, the bishop set out his case for providing a suitable residence for himself in 'the city of Whithorn', where he currently had no personal accommodation. His nearest residence, he claimed, was 12 miles (*c* 19km) from Whithorn, a reference probably to the manor-house at The Clary, north of Wigtown. While he was forced into inconvenient travel to perform his duties, there were a number of properties around the cathedral which belonged to the canons but were unused. Indeed, the bishop claimed that 'there are also not a few streets and lodgings, ruinous, empty and uninhabited', a portion of which could be assigned to him to build a house from which he could enter and exit the cathedral 'similar to episcopal residences in other cities of the realm of Scotland'. It is possible that the result of this appeal was the acquisition of Balnespick or Bishopton (NX 440409) just north-west of the burgh, which is first recorded as episcopal property in 1459.[105]

Evidence for the physical extent of the later medieval town is scanty, but there are records of a number of tenements in the central part of the town possessed by members of its small merchant-burgess community. In 1473, there are records of three tenements on the north side of the market cross.[106] The middle one had been the property of a Wigtown merchant,

John McCrystin, which he had leased to Duncan McCulloch, burgess of Whithorn, at an annual rent of 20s Scots and stabling for two horses when he (John), his heirs or assignees, came to Whithorn 'on business or religion'. A second group of properties adjacent to the Ket burn is recorded in 1481. They comprised a tenement in which the prior infefted the local laird, Blase Vaus of Barnbarroch, bounded on the west by the tenement of the parish clerk, David Robertson, and on the east by the burn.[107] The instrument of sasine was witnessed by three other Whithorn burgesses. A second group of burgesses and their properties emerges in 1495 when Finlay Adair, burgess, resigned his tenement on the north side of the cross into the hands of the prior, who immediately granted it to one James McCulloch.[108] Another group of tenements, also lying to the north of the market cross, is described in a sasine in 1503.[109] The beneficiary was Duncan Murray, already a tenant of one of the flanking tenements. A vennel to one side of Murray's property is described as 'extending from the common highway [George Street] to a certain well between the ends of the said tenements, which vennel has long been closed and out of use'. Whether Murray was seeking to absorb the vennel into his own property or reopen it as a through route from the main street to the burgh fields is unknown. A final group of three tenements lying to the north of the cross is detailed in an instrument in 1550 which narrated the resignation of interest in the principal tenement of Duncan McGown in the burgh by his divorced wife, Margaret McClellane.[110]

With the exception of the one tenement bounded on the east by the Ket, none of the properties referred to can be fixed with certainty. Even the Ket boundary does not tell us on which side of the main street the tenement lay. The orientations given in the sasines are ambiguous (does north side of the cross mean on the northern side of the street or at the northern end of the street?), but the use of the Ket as an eastern boundary seems to indicate that 'north' means the side of the burgh towards the priory rather than geographical north. What seems clear, however, is that the north side of the street was the one most favoured by the principal burgesses in the later fifteenth and early sixteenth centuries, possibly due to the prestige afforded by proximity to the principal gate into the monastic precinct.

Burgh status

Confirmation of Whithorn's status as a free burgh in barony under the prior was granted by King James II in August 1450, when he ratified a recently issued charter of William, 8th Earl of Douglas.[111] This charter probably reiterated the terms of Edward Bruce's original grant, but made some significant additions. He granted the priory 'the whole burgh of Candida Casa and lands lying within the lordship of Galloway, together with the toll of the isle of Portquhitherne'. This was to be held by the prior in free barony and pure and perpetual alms, that is to say for no payment other than the saying of prayers for the donor. This liberty was widened significantly by an award of free regality jurisdiction, which gave the prior the right to hear in his own court even those cases normally reserved for the king's court. Furthermore, the burgesses were granted a wide range of financial and legal privileges and liberties, which might have formed an incentive for further development of the merchant and craft community in Whithorn. In June 1451, while he was attempting to take control of the earldom of Wigtown from the 8th Earl of Douglas, King James regranted the burgh to the prior, to be held directly of the crown, in pure and perpetual alms and free regality.[112] This was not a grant of royal burgh status, however, but a confirmation of its status as a burgh in barony. It was the prior who was being made a direct tenant of the crown, not the burgh. Whithorn's status was reaffirmed in 1459 when James II confirmed the earlier charters following his destruction of the Black Douglas family and annexation of their estates to the crown.

Based on these trading privileges, and the generous provision of additional mercantile rights by James IV in the 1490s (see below), Whithorn's burgesses, with the support of the prior, appear to have extended their operations to a point where they began to have a significant impact on Wigtown's trade. Wigtown, as the established royal burgh, launched an action before the Lords of Council in 1510 intended to halt this trade, which it claimed was contrary to its privileges and rights.[113] The case was continued until 1511, but in the interim, no doubt driven by the threat from Wigtown, Whithorn sought a clarification and reaffirmation of its own charters and trading privileges. The result was a new charter issued by James IV on 1 May 1511. This fresh grant has often been taken as signifying an award of royal burgh status, but it was in fact simply a redefinition, on slightly more generous terms, of the earlier charters.[114] Apart from changing the fair date from late August to late June, and shifting the market day from Saturday to Monday, the main changes were simply clarification of the burgh's right to engage in international trade. Although perhaps enjoying greater privileges than most free burghs, Whithorn was still only a burgh in barony under the superiority of the prior.

The ambiguity in the phrasing of the 1511 charter, however, was to enable the burgesses to claim royal burgh status and stave off the threat to their livelihood and activities from the burgesses of Wigtown in the decades ahead. Recognition of that danger by the burgesses of Wigtown prompted a protest by their alderman before the Lords of Council that the ratification of the charters 'should not turn them nor their freedoms to prejudice'.[115] Throughout the litigation, the case presented by Wigtown was careful to stress that Whithorn was a *town* not a *burgh* and its inhabitants of all ranks were referred to as *indwellers* rather than *burgesses*, language designed to emphasise its inferior status. Their argument, however, was based on the fundamental assumption that as the older, and unequivocally royal, burgh, their rights took precedence over those of Whithorn. Although it is an established fact that Wigtown was the more senior, having held royal burgh status since the mid-thirteenth century, its ability to prove that seniority in court depended on its ability to present parchment evidence.

This was the weakness in their case and Prior Henry of Whithorn may have known that when, in 1512, he offered to show his priory's records to the court and demonstrate that they were older than anything held by Wigtown.[116] In 1518, it was Wigtown which displayed its royal charter, dating from 1457,[117] and, although that had seemed sufficient to establish Wigtown's right, it was actually from that point that its case began to unravel. The Lords of Council found against Whithorn on the strength of the 1457 charter and the non-appearance in court of Whithorn's representatives, but any feeling of triumph in Wigtown must have quickly evaporated and the record of the court's decision was formally cancelled. In March 1519 Whithorn's procurator in the case pounced, asking for a formal registration of the date of Wigtown's charter, which post-dated their own charter from Robert I.[118] Wigtown all but recognised that the case was lost and had begun to negotiate for a compromise some days earlier. A representative for Edinburgh at the proceedings requested that it should be noted formally that if Whithorn was to be admitted as a free burgh then it should be on the strength of its earlier possession of that status before the grant to Wigtown. The case records then fall silent.

By 1531, some twelve years later, it appears that Whithorn's status as a royal burgh had been recognised implicitly, for in that year it was taxed with the other Scottish burghs. Burghs negotiated over the proportion of the assessment each would make, Whithorn agreeing to pay £6.[119] In the same tax assessment, Wigtown paid £7, reflecting perhaps its continued greater importance as a trading centre at this time, but more probably a question of burgh pride and determination to be seen to be able to pay more than their upstart neighbour. Whithorn's contribution was, however, the equal of burghs like Elgin and Selkirk, and higher than Crail (£4), Kirkcaldy (£5 10s), Dunbar (£4), Lauder (£4), Peebles (£5), or Rutherglen (£4). While definitely in the lower league of burghs in comparison to places like Haddington, which contributed £18, Whithorn was evidently deemed to be prospering. Whithorn's participation in the convention which agreed and apportioned the tax may have been the trigger for a revival of the proceedings with Wigtown in December 1532, in which the dates of the respective charters seem again to have been the main issue.[120] In February 1533, Wigtown's claims were dismissed 'because the crown and Wigtoun had not verified nor proved the points thereof'.[121]

Recognition of royal burgh status brought obligations and burdens as well as privileges. In 1599, for example, Whithorn was among the south-western burghs charged with providing men for a military force to be led by the Earl of Angus against reivers and outlaws in the West March. Each burgh was to provide a number of hagbutters, complete with sufficient powder and bullets, proportionate to their relative size and wealth as communities. The largest burghs, Dumfries and Kirkcudbright, provided 40 and 20 respectively, Wigtown was to provide 14, while Whithorn was commanded to provide only 6 men, suggesting the town was already in decline.[122]

Pilgrimage, royal and public

Pilgrimage to St Ninian's shrine was apparently a well-established tradition from at least the Northumbrian period (eighth to ninth centuries), when the saint's cult appears first to have been promoted (**fig 22**), but Whithorn does not feature among the favoured pilgrimage destinations of Scottish or English rulers and nobles until the fourteenth century, although poor survival of earlier documentation may have skewed that picture. The first recorded high-status pilgrim to the shrine was Edward, Prince of Wales, the future Edward II of England, who visited Whithorn during his father's campaign in southern Scotland in 1301. It was reported to Edward I that the Scots, learning of the prince's planned pilgrimage, had taken the main image of St Ninian from the priory to Sweetheart Abbey, south of Dumfries, but it had miraculously transported itself back to Whithorn overnight in time to receive its royal visitor.[123]

The earliest recorded Scottish royal pilgrim was Robert I, who, during the last months of his life in spring 1329, made a slow progress from his manor-house at Cardross on the Clyde, down through Carrick to Innermessan/Inchmichael, Glenluce, Monreith and Whithorn.[124] Robert was perhaps seeking a cure from the debilitating wasting disease which had afflicted him, and was possibly also seeking final absolution from Galloway's saint for the terrible harrying which he had unleashed on the province two decades earlier. After 1332, renewed Anglo-Scottish and civil warfare, in which Galloway became a major theatre of conflict, ended royal pilgrimages to the shrine, and although peace was restored in 1357 it was not until the late fifteenth century that Scottish royalty again visited Whithorn.

Pilgrim traffic may have been affected adversely by Anglo-Scottish hostilities for much of the fourteenth and early fifteenth century, despite Bishop Elisaeus's claim of 'great multitudes' coming there in 1408. In the period of renewed stability which followed James I's release in 1424 from his long captivity in England, however, the flow of visitors had either increased or was expected to increase. In December 1428 the king issued a general licence to all English and Manx pilgrims wishing to visit the shrine, granting them safe and secure passage through Galloway overland from the east or by sea from Man.[125] They were permitted to remain in Scotland for a maximum of fifteen days and, on the route to Whithorn, were to wear one designated token and to receive a second one from the prior for the return journey, both to be worn openly on their clothing. While in Scotland, they were to conduct themselves

FIGURE 22
This carved oak figure of a
bishop was found in a moss
near Whithorn and dates
from the fourteenth century.
It may represent St Ninian
(© Trustees of the National
Museums of Scotland)

only as pilgrims with permission to buy such as was needful for their travels, but they were to engage in neither trade nor diplomatic negotiations. Royal protections and edicts, however, were not always sufficient to protect pilgrims from England, as a payment of 14s in 1504 from James IV to an unfortunate English couple reveals. The pair, who had been coming via the landward route from the east, had been 'spulzeit' (robbed) by an Englishman and a Scotsman.[126]

Apart from the evidence for royal pilgrims to Whithorn discussed below, there is surprisingly little evidence for the nature and level of pilgrim traffic from within Scotland. One of the earliest references occurs in an anonymous late fourteenth-century Life of St Ninian written in Scots by someone who was clearly familiar with local politics and the nature of the shrine at Whithorn.[127] It mentions pilgrims arriving from France, Spain, England, Wales and Ireland in great numbers (although the figure given of 10,000 is surely an exaggeration), seeking mainly cures of bodily ailments.[128] A series of late fourteenth-century miracles performed by Ninian are recounted in this Life. One was the cure of the infected leg of John Balormy, who had journeyed from Elgin in Moray, and the manner in which the tale is presented indicates that such cure-seeking pilgrimages were already commonplace by the period when the work was written (c 1360–75).[129] A supplication was sent to Pope Eugenius IV in 1440–41 from Margaret, countess of Douglas, asking that indulgences be granted to the pious who made contributions towards the building costs of a stone bridge over the River Bladnoch near Wigtown.[130] The appeal suggests that a significant volume of pilgrim traffic was using this land route from the north, sufficient to merit the replacement of the existing timber bridge over the river – which suffered frequent damage from floods – with a more substantial stone structure. There is also a suggestion that bodies of pilgrims congregated at the river-crossing, possibly for some kind of more organised procession down the remaining ten miles of road to the shrine.

No indication is given of who these pilgrims were or where they originated, but among them were individuals seeking forgiveness for very worldly (as opposed to spiritual) crimes. By the later fifteenth century Whithorn was given as one of the four 'head shrines' of the kingdom to which convicted homicides were obliged to undertake penitential pilgrimages.[131] Its later recorded success in attracting high-status pilgrims, however, suggests that it was equally successful in drawing less-exalted individuals from across Scotland. This is hinted at, for example, in the record of 14d given as alms by James IV to 'pur folkis of Tayn passand to Quhithirn', whom he encountered on the road in Ayrshire when returning from his own pilgrimage to Whithorn.[132] Why he felt moved to give these poor folk alms rather than any of the many others whom he surely encountered, other than a sense of affinity founded on his own devotion to St Duthac of Tain, can only be guessed at.

It is the high-status visitors rather than the poor pilgrims who underline the importance of the shrine in the late medieval period. In the summer of 1473 Margaret of Denmark, queen of James III, visited the shrine, probably to pray for a successful outcome to her pregnancy.[133] It was their son, James IV, who developed the strongest associations with the shrine, beginning in August 1488, only six weeks after the end of the rebellion which had seen the death of his father at Sauchieburn, when he sent Sir John Towers to make a money offering to St Ninian, probably as a penance.[134] The king's regular visits to the shrine began in November 1491 and, like his almost-annual pilgrimages to the shrine of St Duthac at Tain, were perhaps as much political as spiritual in motivation, providing him with the opportunity to see and be seen in peripheral areas of the kingdom where royal power had been remote and often ineffective for most of the fourteenth and fifteenth centuries.[135] The 1491 trip was certainly not a pious, self-denying act on the young king's part: Saturday 12 November was spent playing – and losing – at cards with members of his retinue. Subsequent visits also reveal a mingling of pious activity with pleasure. In 1498, for example, alongside the £6 8s which he gave to priests for masses at Whithorn and the £4 5s 6d given as offerings to St Ninian, he gave 11s 8d to 'young Rudman', the lutar, and 14d 'to ane dwerch wif' (a dwarf woman) who entertained him during his stay, while in 1501 he rewarded the prior's lutar and John Hopringle, a trumpeter.[136] That latter year he appears also to have been accompanied by his falconer, and in 1502 payment was made for the recovery of a hawk which had flown off during the journey to Whithorn.[137] In 1506–07, payments were made to lutars [lute-players], the prior's clarsachd-player [Gaelic harp-player], four Italian minstrels who entertained the king and queen on the road between Whithorn and Tongland, a tabronar [drummer] and his 'marrow' [companion], and two trumpeters.[138] In 1501, however, the greatest expense was in payments for fitting out his mistress's wardrobe and horse-gear for her pilgrimage of thanksgiving after the birth of their son James Stewart, later Earl of Moray.[139]

The financial records of James IV's 1491 pilgrimage hint at the preparations behind such occasions, and concern at the possible inability of Whithorn and places along the way readily to accommodate the royal retinue. On 30 October he sent a messenger ahead from Linlithgow to ensure that adequate provision was made for his arrival, presumably to ensure that there were both suitable lodgings and sufficient victuals for the king and his attendants for a number of days.[140] Large-scale pilgrimages involving even just the core of the king's household could not have been spontaneous events but minor campaigns which entailed significant logistical preparations. In 1497 and 1505, for example, the king's Master Cook was among the personnel who accompanied him, and in 1498 payment was made on route to the royal kitchen lads, suggesting that the household was perhaps not intending to rely on what fare could be provided for them in inns and lodgings along the road.[141] From 1496 James began to visit the shrine on an almost annual basis, sometimes riding alone, as on his famous 1507 express trip to Tain, or with just a small retinue. He travelled by a number of routes: in September 1497, for example, he came south via Biggar, Durrisdeer, St John's Town of Dalry, and Wigtown, returning north to Glasgow through Ayr and Kilmarnock, while in April 1498 he came from Dumbarton via Ayr and Ballantrae.[142] This western route, through Ayr and apparently down the Cree valley, was the most favoured one, but the route from the east through Dumfries and Kirkcudbright was also taken, as in May 1503.[143]

During his pilgrimages, James made significant payments as offerings or for masses said on his behalf. In April 1501, he offered £4 18s at the shrine, relics and altars in the cathedral-priory, while in August of the same year he made offerings of £3 10s, and payments of £4 to the canons and £3 to priests, presumably for masses.[144] In 1503, in addition to these types of devotional payment, he also gave money to be distributed by his almoner,[145] and he paid for masses to be said for specific individuals, such as that offered in June 1504 for 'Mastres Helenor'.[146] Like a normal pilgrim to the shrine, however, James also purchased 'takinnis of Sanct Niniane' (tokens or pilgrim's badges), perhaps similar to one now in Dumfries Museum (**fig 23**).[147] His two largest offerings were made in 1506, when 'ane relique quhilk the King offerit at Quhithirn maid of the Kingis aun silvir' was left at the shrine, and 1508, when he left another reliquary worth £17 12d.[148] The first reliquary was fashioned from 27½ ounces of silver, and was gilded with mercury and gold from two English gold nobles (coins worth 6s 8d each), materials and work coming to £8 14s. This was a striking display of royal devotion to Ninian, but was considerably overshadowed by the 83¼ ounces of his own silver used in having reliquaries made for the shrine of St Duthac at Tain.[149]

After 1508, evidence for annual pilgrimages to Whithorn in the Treasurer's Accounts ceases and during the last five years of his life James seems to have directed most of his devotional activity towards Tain. The years 1491 to 1508 appear to have been Whithorn's apogee as a royal pilgrimage destination, for there was no re-emergence of the shrine as a favoured pilgrimage destination in the reign of James V. In 1526, expensive plans had been made to bring the young king to Whithorn,[150] but the political turmoil in the kingdom at the time led to the abandonment of the scheme. There is no clear evidence that James V ever made a formal pilgrimage to Whithorn during his adult reign. Unlike his father, his demonstrations of personal piety were altogether less charismatic and he showed no great interest in devotion to particular saints' cults or in undertaking pilgrimages. It was not simply an aversion to Whithorn, for Tain also ceased to enjoy the benefits of regular royal visits after the death of James IV. James V made only one pilgrimage to Tain, in 1534, an act which effectively brought down the curtain on the Scottish crown's public displays of veneration for saints' cults in the pre-Reformation period. When his daughter, Queen Mary, visited Whithorn on 10–11 August 1563, it was a largely social and political event and there is no evidence that she attempted to make any offering at the shrine, from which the relics had in any case already been removed.[151] Long before devotional pilgrimage and the cult of saints were formally proscribed by parliament in 1581, the flow of pilgrim traffic to Whithorn had probably already dried up.

FIGURE 23
Pilgrim token made of lead and found in excavation spoil at Whithorn. The holes allowed it to be sewn to the clothing of the pilgrim, as was Scottish and continental practice. It shows a bishop holding a crook and giving a blessing, and only the head is missing, but there is insufficient evidence to be certain it represents St Ninian (© Dumfries and Galloway Museums Service)

Post-Reformation Whithorn, *c* 1560–1638

The Reformation had an immediate impact on Whithorn. Bishop Alexander Gordon, who had only been nominated to the see in 1559 and was reluctant to lose his position after years of struggling to secure such a lucrative office, made a swift declaration of support for Protestantism.[152] His lead was followed by a majority of the remaining canons, six or seven of whom were to serve as readers or ministers in the reformed Church after 1560. Unlike the bishop, who was rarely to visit his cathedral, these men – and their fellows who continued to adhere to Roman Catholicism – may have continued to reside in the priory for the remainder of their lives, and continued to receive their share of the monastic revenue. Despite the efforts of Prior Malcolm Fleming to maintain some form of Catholic worship at Whithorn, the proscription of the mass in the Reformation Parliament of 1560 had effectively rendered the cathedral church, with its multiplicity of chapels and altars, largely redundant. While the nave of the cathedral, which had probably always served as the parish church, appears to have been retained, the transepts and eastern limb of the building may swiftly have fallen into disrepair. Indeed, it appears that by *c* 1600 most of the medieval church was already a largely roofless ruin.[153]

Given that the bishops of Whithorn had probably rarely been resident for much of the later medieval period, the most noticeable impact on the burgh was probably the loss of many of the ancillary functions associated with a pre-Reformation diocesan centre, rather than the disappearance of bishops per se. One significant loss was the consistory, the bishop's court which had jurisdiction over moral and spiritual matters, particularly matrimonial and executry cases. The regular sessions of that court, probably in a building attached to the cathedral-priory, would have provided employment for specialist lawyers and brought additional revenue into the burgh from those attending it.

Under the new Protestant regime, consistories were replaced in 1564 by a single commissary court based at Edinburgh, which dealt with all matrimonial issues, and testaments above a certain value. Lesser cases were delegated to commissary courts based on the old dioceses or 'commissariots'. Whithorn, as the former diocesan centre, might have expected to become the meeting-place of the new commissariot of Galloway, but by 1575, if not earlier, the new court was meeting at Wigtown, probably in recognition of its already pre-eminent regional role as a legal centre and meeting-place of the sheriff court.[154] This was an economic blow as much as a loss of prestige, but it was swiftly compounded by the disappearance of another beneficial feature of the old regime, its role as the meeting-place of the diocesan synod. These gatherings of the diocesan clergy under the leadership of the bishop, although less frequent than meetings of the consistory, would have drawn in senior clerics and important lay officials from around the diocese, all of whom would have required accommodation within the burgh and been significant spenders during their stays there. The loss of such high-status gatherings would have had a particular impact on niche segments of the burgh's economy. Whithorn might have expected, as the former diocesan centre, to have become the venue for the regional assemblies of the new Protestant ministers, the 'presbytery'. When the system was proposed in 1581 Whithorn was the designated venue, but when the new system was finally instituted in 1588, the local presbytery, like the commissary court, met in Wigtown.[155] There can have been few clearer statements of Whithorn's loss of relevance in the post-1560 political-religious order in Scotland.

Perhaps more immediately crippling was the banning of religious pilgrimages in 1581. For a community which had grown up and flourished through the provision of services to the pilgrims visiting St Ninian's shrine, the final ban removed the principal *raison d'être* for the burgh. The numbers of pilgrims to Whithorn had probably been declining steadily from the 1530s, particularly after the beginning of the Reformation in England in 1532, but the continued adherence to Roman Catholicism of several prominent local families in Galloway, such as the Stewarts of Garlies and the Maxwells, had perhaps helped to maintain traditional forms of devotion.

Feuds between local lairds contributed to a growing air of decline in the burgh in the closing decade of the sixteenth century. A long-running dispute between the Murrays of Broughton and the Ahannays of Sorbie saw a series of skirmishes, minor raids, assaults, woundings and killings between July 1598 and July 1600. On occasion these spilled over into the burgh, as in the case of the attempted murder of George Murray of Broughton in March 1598 when he was going to church in Whithorn, and a later assault in the town on one of his tenants.[156]

That all was not well in the burgh is indicated by the record in 1603 of the legal denunciation of John Gowyne, provost of Whithorn, on unspecified charges brought by Uhtred MacDowall of Mundork, and the cautioning of Alexander Stewart of Garlies to the tune of £1000 not to 'reset or intercommune' with Gowyne.[157] The greatest of the neighbouring landowners, Alexander Stewart, Lord Garlies, and his wide network of kin in the southern Machars, was also involved in low-level criminality and acts of violence. A dispute in 1617 between Garlies and William Clugstoun, burgess of Whithorn, started with an assault on and wounding of Clugstoun on his lands near the burgh. Clugstoun fled by sea to Kirkcudbright, but was pursued by Garlies and his men, after they had broken into and ransacked Clugstoun's house in Whithorn.[158]

In the midst of these local feuds and upheavals, the religious state of the kingdom was also undergoing protracted dissolution and reformation. King James VI had moved progressively in the 1590s towards the restoration of some kind of episcopal and diocesan structure to the Scottish Church and, after his move to England in 1603 and exposure to the full-blown episcopacy of the Anglican Church, set about a formal re-establishment of an episcopal regime in Scotland. In 1605, Gavin Hamilton was appointed bishop of Whithorn, and by 1606 had regained from the crown the lands and revenues of his pre-Reformation predecessors, augmented by the annexed revenues of the priory.[159] Hamilton was only consecrated in October 1610 and was dead by February 1612, but it is possible that he was the man responsible for initiating the refit of the ruinous medieval cathedral as a cathedral church for the restored diocese, although it is perhaps more likely to have been his successor, William Couper (1612–19).[160] A Dutch/Flemish bell bearing the date 1610 probably relates to this refurbishing of the priory church as the cathedral for the newly reinstated diocese.[161] It appears that only the nave of the medieval church was reused, reflecting perhaps both the already ruined state of the old liturgical east end, and also the understated form of worship practised by these first reformed bishops. Hamilton and Couper may have been responsible for the building of a western tower on the nave to replace the belfry that had probably once stood over the crossing of the medieval church, and the construction of a screen wall to fill the void where the nave had opened into the crossing, but their architectural intervention was otherwise limited.

In 1635, however, Thomas Sydserf was appointed as bishop. Sydserf embraced the elaborate ritual which Charles I wished to introduce to the Church in Scotland, and set out to provide his cathedral with the desired physical layout for the new liturgy. Ralegh Radford's excavations after 1949 revealed what may have been Sydserf's scheme for a formalised liturgical east end to the church, with an altar in front of the eastern screen wall. The upper part of this wall was pierced by a large pointed-headed window which would have lit the reinstated chancel area, while in the south wall a new doorway was inserted using a fine later fifteenth-century opening salvaged from elsewhere in the ruinous complex, and a twelfth-century archway was inserted further west in the south wall.[162] Sydserf clearly intended to visit his cathedral, and may have envisaged the setting up of a formal chapter of resident canons to serve there, but there is no evidence for more than the parish minister. As a result, there was no move towards the provision of manses for cathedral clergy, or a house for the bishop himself. The 'cathedral' remained effectively an elaborate parish church standing in isolation amidst the ruins of the medieval priory complex, with only the manse for the minister and (post-1633) parish schoolhouse occupied. Sydserf's arrangements were short-lived, for in 1638 the Episcopalian regime was overthrown with the beginning of the Covenanting movement, and although episcopacy was restored in 1660 there is no evidence that a functioning cathedral was reinstated at Whithorn.

Isle of Whithorn

The first certain reference to the Isle is in the 1325 charter of Robert I, which confirmed his younger brother Edward Bruce's grants of burgh status to Whithorn, and rights to the tolls of the 'Isle of Port Whithorn'.[163] Apart from the repetition of that award in subsequent confirmations of the fourteenth-century charter, and the inference that trade was being carried on by the burgesses of Whithorn (see below), there is no clear reference to a functioning port or any settlement at Isle of Whithorn until the early 1500s. The 'chapel on the hill', at which James IV made offerings in 1501 and the years following, is probably the chapel beside the landing-place at the Isle, a possibly thirteenth-century structure built for pilgrims to make offerings in thanks for their safe arrival.[164] It is likely that it was into the haven at the Isle that the ships carrying King James V and Sir James Hamilton of Finnart were driven on their western expedition in July 1536 when hit by 'tempest and contrarious wyndis' and compelled to land in 'Quhytheirne'.[165] Clearly it was a port known to skippers sailing west-coast waters.

After the Reformation, the priory's lands and revenues at the Isle were simply commodities to be alienated or feued as necessary. The Isle itself comprised a significant block of property, valued in 1569 as a 5-merkland.[166] Nine years later, the mails (rents) and duties of the Isle were assigned as the main portion of an annual pension of £50 given by Robert Stewart, commendator of Whithorn, to one Patrick Sharp, the first in a series of such pensions drawn on the priory revenues.[167] The division of the Isle into tenancies, suggesting the existence of a small community at the port, emerges in 1587, when John Martin senior and John Martin junior, tenants of the 'Inner Yle', complained in a letter to Patrick Sharp's father, John, that they were 'havelie molestit' in their possession by one John McGowne.[168] Sharp and the Martins had been in dispute from as early as 1584 over their withholding of the teinds of his 5 merklands of the Isle,[169] and the 'molestation' appears to have been connected with that dispute. In 1595, Sharp and the Martins entered into a contract whereby Sharp disponed 'an equal half' of his 5 merklands and assigned to them the tack of the teinds which he held.[170]

The port at the Isle assumed a brief political importance in the 1570s and 1580s when it served as one of the conduits through which supporters of Queen Mary, particularly Lords Fleming and Herries, Gordon of Lochinvar, Stewart of Garlies and Kennedy of Bargany, maintained their spy networks and diplomatic connections with France, Spain and the Papacy. It was possibly to the Isle that Lord Livingston sailed from Dumfries in 1570, when he 'landed beside Whitehorn',[171] and it was perhaps the harbour which served Lord Fleming, Lord Herries and Gordon of Lochinvar in 1572 when Fleming sailed by the 'wost seis' (west seas) to join with his confederates at Cruggleton Castle.[172] In February 1590, the arrival at the 'Ile of Quhithorne' of a Spanish galley provoked great consternation.[173] The Spaniards had, they claimed, been undertaking a reconnaissance voyage to determine the condition of the English navy and gain intelligence in advance of another naval assault on England, but had been driven up through the Irish Sea towards Galloway, where they had taken refuge at the Isle. It was suspected, however, that the captain had also been in communication with Catholic lords in the south-west, most notably Lord Maxwell, pointing again to the value of the secluded haven as a place through which to undertake clandestine business.

Trade

Evidence for significant overseas trade being undertaken by Whithorn-based merchants is fragmentary. The earliest surviving record is in a petition dated *c* 1451–52 submitted to John Kemp, cardinal-archbishop of York.[174] In it, four Whithorn merchants complained that in the previous June they had freighted a ship of La Rochelle with a cargo consisting mainly of salt (42 tuns) and wine (12 tuns), plus various smaller items of higher value, including bales of Breton linen and five feather beds, worth over £90 in total. The ship, however, heading for 'the port of Whithorn *alias* Wigtown', had been seized by an English vessel off the Welsh coast, the goods seized and the petitioners imprisoned in Pembroke Castle despite the current Anglo-Scottish truce. The outcome of the petition is unknown. What is most interesting is that there were groups of merchants operating out of Whithorn on perhaps a joint-stock basis. They did not possess vessels of their own, but were hiring ships as necessary or, perhaps, the cargo they were importing was larger than could be carried in one of their own vessels. The reference to Wigtown as 'the port of Whithorn' is interesting, as, if not a mistake, it suggests that the regional royal burgh may have been successful in halting trade through the Isle.

By the later fifteenth century the prior and canons were themselves trading actively, perhaps exporting some of the surpluses produced on the monastic estate or received as rents from their tenants. To assist and encourage them, in January 1492 James IV granted Prior Patrick Vaus and the canons the custom of all types of goods which they were carrying in their own ships into or from Scottish ports.[175] The implication is that not only were they active in foreign trade but they were also operating their own ships, possibly from the Isle. The 1492 grant was confirmed in a slightly fuller form in 1499, detailing the goods intended in the grant as hides, wool, skins, cloths, and fish.[176] Interestingly, there is no mention of salt, which formed the bulk of the 1451–52 cargo and was an important customable commodity.

These grants still stopped short of giving Whithorn the full trading privileges of a royal burgh, but it appears that the prior and burgesses chose to interpret them very loosely. Their activities quickly aroused the anger of the burgesses of Wigtown, who in June 1510 launched a legal challenge against their smaller rival, accusing them of 'wrongfully usurping and using the privileges of [Wigtown] and defrauding the crown of the customs in the drawing of strangers and their ships from the burgh and freedom thereof to the Isle of Quhitherne'.[177] It was probably this threat which encouraged the burgesses of Whithorn to seek a stronger affirmation of their rights; this was secured by a fresh charter granted in 1511 by James IV.[178] Among the accusations made by Wigtown's representatives in 1513 was the allegation that Whithorn had been trafficking with Englishmen, Irishmen and Manxmen during times of hostility between the kingdoms. Five or six young men of the town, it was said, had taken puncheons of wine to Man; the prior of Whithorn admitted that he and his men traded with Irishmen and Manxmen. Twelve 'indwellers' of Whithorn, including a bailie of the town, were accused of diverting various ships that had been coming to Wigtown to Isle of Whithorn instead, buying their cargos and selling wine, salt and wool to English merchants.[179] The scale of their success was set out in charges made in January 1517 that in 1513 and 1514 they had diverted two ships from Wigtown each year, and three in both 1515 and 1516.[180] The ships were described as French and Breton and laden with Gascon wine, iron, salt and other merchandise, which was sold off in small parcels to the English, Irish and Manx.

In the winter of 1494–95, the dangers of the coast around Burrow Head were underscored by the wrecking of a ship there. The vessel appears to have been particularly valuable, for the king took a special interest in it, despatching a herald with letters of instruction to the sheriff of Wigtown 'anentis the schip at brak at Quhithirne'.[181] In 1584 and again in the winter of 1589/90, stormy weather was the cause of unexpected ships arriving in the haven at the Isle. The first was a vessel carrying personal possessions of the exiled Earl of Mar from Ireland to England, including a rich collection of clothing which was gifted to Thomas Stewart, brother of Lord Garlies, and William Houston of Cutreoch, who had apprehended Mar's servitor, John Duncan, 'with the saidis goodis and claythis within the bounds of the ile of Quhithorne, quha wes be storm of weddir drevin in thairintill'.[182] The second was the Spanish galley mentioned earlier. Piracy, however, appears to have been a greater threat than storms to vessels operated by Whithorn merchants, as the 1451 petition above indicates. In May 1522, Duncan McGown, burgess of Whithorn, who was trading in partnership with two Ayr merchants, was 'taken upon the sey' by an English ship and all three were carried as prisoners to England. A court action launched by Duncan in February 1523 against his former partners revealed that he had remained in England as pledge for the others while they returned to Scotland to raise their ransoms, but that they had abandoned him there, and he had languished in prison for eleven weeks until he raised the money to pay all three ransoms. McGown's ill-fortune continued in 1525–26, when a ship of his laden with 'herring and fish' was seized by an Englishman in Loch Ryan.[183] This appears to confirm the suggestion made in 1451 that at least some of Whithorn's merchants were operating out of ports other than the Isle.

Whithorn's burgesses were not just victims of English piracy but also beneficiaries. On 21 September 1577, two English merchants complained before the Privy Council that another Englishman, 'Andro Quhyte piratt', had in 1565 seized three of their fully laden ships valued at £400 sterling and had sold them and their cargos at the port of Whithorn.[184] The record reveals how the goods were sold to a network of lairds, clerics, burgesses and small tenants in the southern Machars area, headed by Patrick McGown, provost of Whithorn, who took 19 puncheons of wine and 100lbs of 'plum damus' from the cargo. Three other burgesses of Whithorn and six indwellers were among the individuals involved in disposing of the goods.

The coastal movement of shipping along the Galloway coast, including the port at the Isle, is implicit in the evidence for eastern Galloway and Dumfriesshire stone employed in the cathedral buildings at various stages from the twelfth to the sixteenth century.[185] It is unlikely that bulky commodities such as stone were moved by land, particularly when both the quarries and the end-users were sited close to the sea. Documented movement of shipping along the coast, however, does not survive before the sixteenth century. In 1570, it was reported that Lord Livingston had embarked at Dumfries and 'landed beside Whitehorn in Galloway', presumably at the Isle.[186] In 1617, the flight of William Clugstoun, burgess of Whithorn, from Alexander Stewart of Garlies and his henchmen by boat to Kirkcudbright suggests again that short-distance movement along the Solway and Irish Sea coasts was not uncommon.[187] Evidence for Whithorn's involvement in local and regional sea-borne trade is clearer in the early seventeenth century. In 1602, unnamed Whithorn traders were among the 'wretchit catives and unworthy personis' of the western coastal burghs between Glasgow and Kirkcudbright who 'preferring thair unlauchfull and privat gayne to a guid conscience' had continued to trade with rebels who were fighting against the English government in Ireland.[188] The Scottish government appears to have struggled to monitor the trading activities of west-coast merchants, perhaps especially through the smaller and remoter ports, and the few recorded instances of action being taken against individuals for illicit trade probably represent only the visible tip of a very large iceberg which otherwise avoided detection. The Privy Council's action in 1604 to recover custom payable on 10 tuns of wine landed at the Isle by two Ayr merchants and a south Lanarkshire laird looks very like an isolated detection of what was a quite common occurrence.[189]

Control of trade through the south-western ports, particularly with Ireland, continued to be a problem for the authorities in Scotland through the seventeenth century. Legislation was introduced in 1616 to control the Irish trade by issuing passports and permits for the movement of people, cattle and victuals from Ireland into west-coast ports, but the system appears to have been largely ineffectual. One particular concern in the 1620s was that Scottish merchants were importing cheaper produce from Ireland, mainly wheat and barley, undercutting the fixed prices for domestic produce and thereby harming domestic producers.[190] Along with the other regional trading centres, Whithorn was enjoined in 1626 by the Privy Council to desist from such unregulated trade which was further damaging the Scottish economy. Licensed trade was permitted, but only through designated ports. In 1627 Hugh Montgomery, Viscount Airds, received a warrant from the king to issue such licences, with the three Galloway ports authorised to conduct trade with Ireland named as Kirkcudbright, Portpatrick and Whithorn.[191] Why Wigtown, which had been named in the earlier legislation, was not listed in the 1627 warrant is unknown, for its port was still functioning.

By the later 1600s, Whithorn's maritime trade appears to have been in sharp decline, possibly in the face of growing local competition. The scale of shipping from the Isle is perhaps indicated by Whithorn's assessed contribution towards a levy of 500 seamen required for royal service in 1672. Whithorn and Wigtown were to provide one seaman each, Portpatrick and Stranraer two men each.[192] Portpatrick, which had become the main port for the Irish trade, with the costs of its development underwritten with royal support from revenues raised,[193] had been gradually rising in importance through the century. The emergence of Stranraer as a second regional port of greater significance than either Whithorn or Wigtown points to a radical realignment of trade patterns towards the western extremity of Galloway.

Covenant to Union, 1638–1707

The signing of the National Covenant and the overthrow of episcopacy in Scotland in the Glasgow Assembly of 1638 may not have been as serious a blow to Whithorn as the events of 1560. Although the burgh was the nominal seat of the Bishop of Galloway and the location of his cathedral, there had been no re-establishment of a substantial ecclesiastical presence whose removal would have had an adverse impact upon the local economy in the way that the demise of the priory and shrine had done in the sixteenth century. Beyond a parish church that was rather large and elaborate for a comparatively small community, there was no institutional structure of diocesan courts, bishop's household, or college of canons, whose presence had previously helped to stimulate and maintain the burgh's economy. Apart from the change in the form of worship, which saw the deliberate obliteration of the liturgical arrangements introduced in Bishop Sydserf's refurbishment of the priory nave, there may have been few visible signs of the religious revolution which had occurred.

Whithorn's increasingly marginal status through the seventeenth century is evident in its absence from any significant part in two decades of civil war, political revolution and military conquest after 1638. It did, however, lie in an area of staunch support for the Presbyterian church system which had been reintroduced to Scotland in 1638. When Charles II returned from his Continental exile in 1660 following the death of Oliver Cromwell and the collapse of the Commonwealth regime, the Scots had expected him to adhere to the promises he had given to maintain the Presbyterian form of worship. Instead, he reneged on his acceptance of the National Covenant and re-established episcopacy. The consequence was three decades of religious conflict, passive and armed resistance by Covenanter supporters of the Presbyterian system, and alternating phases of governmental repression and conciliation. Galloway in general was a centre of opposition to the Episcopalian Church and, although the parish church of Whithorn once again became the nominal cathedral of the see, there is little evidence that it formed any kind of focus for religious activity or church government under the new regime. As had happened before 1638, the main church courts and committees assembled in Wigtown, and the bishops of Galloway appear rarely to have visited the seat of their see.

Hostility to Charles II's designs was met with harsh penalties, including punitive fines designed to break the resistance of leading opposition figures. The four years after 1660 saw the economic ruin of the area, with revenues drained away as so many people were paying fines, compounded by the burden of paying for the local quartering of the troops who were intended to enforce compliance with government policy. Whithorn complained to parliament because it was 'depauperated by the quarterings of three troops of English horse'.[194] The financial crisis was exacerbated by an economic recession: trade in Whithorn was at a standstill.

To ensure that the incumbent Presbyterian ministers were compliant with the new regime, they were supposed to obtain confirmation of their suitability from their bishop. The response throughout Scotland was variable, but in the diocese of Galloway every pre-1660 minister refused to get his appointment confirmed. Accordingly, they were deprived of their livings, forbidden to conduct services and required to leave their manses. Many, however, remained in their parishes and soon were involved in leading illegal religious assemblies known as 'conventicles'. Conventicles started in Kirkpatrick-Durham in Kirkcudbrightshire, and spread throughout the diocese. The bishops responded by appointing alternative ministers, but most were poorly qualified curates, because the pool of properly qualified divines from which to choose was small.

In 1663 an Act was passed requiring Sunday church attendance. Troops were sent to enforce it, and to raid the conventicles. They could impose instant fines, and, if these were not paid, property could be confiscated. The high-handed behaviour of the government's military and religious officials in Galloway was bitterly resented, and in 1666 the ill-treatment of a group of

Presbyterian sympathisers suspected of involvement in conventicles triggered a local rebellion known as the Pentland Rising. The rebels captured the local military commander, Sir James Turner, and marched on Edinburgh in an attempt to force the government to listen to their grievances. Pursued by a government army led by Sir Thomas Dalyell, and having failed to attract widespread support, the rebels turned back within sight of Edinburgh and were eventually defeated and dispersed in a short battle at Rullion Green near Penicuik.[195] Despite the defeat of the rising, the government was unable to impose its religious settlement with any greater effect, and resorted to even more severe repression and fines. In Galloway, these measures financially crippled many middle-ranking families and may have brought further economic decline to the already struggling burgh at Whithorn. Gradually, however, the government had to admit defeat. In 1669 the ministers were allowed back if they agreed to keep the peace. In Wigtownshire only four accepted these terms, although eight more had returned by 1672. After this, more severe punishments were introduced for holding conventicles, and there were some retaliatory assaults on Episcopal curates. In 1678 troops were again sent in, under Claverhouse. The following year the Covenanters were defeated at the battle of Bothwell Bridge. The Test Act was passed in 1681, and persecution and summary justice continued, a period known as the 'killing times'.

In the medieval period the burgh had had 'a good importation trade with France, which brought the merchants of the inland towns to Whithorn for the supply of goods'. According to M'Kerlie, booths had stood in the centre of the main street, but 'after the Reformation the burgh sunk almost into absolute decay. Without trade or foreign intercourse, it became a mere rural village'.[196] In 1684 its Saturday markets were 'not at all frequented', and it was 'a town of little or no trade at present, although of old it was a town of great trade, and resort'.[197]

Evidence for rig and furrow on the fields surrounding the priory has been identified in several excavations. It overlies medieval remains and indicates that the outer margins of the medieval priory were probably taken for agricultural land shortly after the Reformation. The priory itself fell into disrepair and was robbed of stonework for reuse in construction within the town, though the nave survived as the parish kirk. One old building, known as the commendator's house, survived in use as the manse and subsequently partly as the parish school, but its origins are unknown.

The economic decline, which the deteriorating physical condition of the burgh at this time probably reflects, is paralleled in the community's fiscal records. Whithorn's contribution to the Convention's tax roll was insignificant (see **table 1**), dropping from 1% in 1535 to 0.05% by 1705. The new tax roll for the royal burghs drawn up in 1683–84 demonstrates the dwindling significance of Whithorn. Assessed at 2s while Wigtown's contribution was

	1535		1597		1612		1649		1670		1690		1705	
	£	%	£	%	£	%	£	%	£	%	£	%	£	%
Ayr	78 15s	2.4	2 3s 4d	2.2	216 13s 4d	2.2	1 8s	1.4	1 14s 8d	1.7	1 14s 8d	1.7	1 1s 4d	1.06
Dumfries	41 5s	1.2	1 16s 8d	1.7	183 6s 8d	1.8	1 13s 4d	1.7	1 13s 4d	1.7	1 18s 4d	1.9	1 18s 4d	1.9
Irvine	45	1.4	1 4s	1.2	120	1.2	1	1	18s	0.9	18s	0.9	10s 6d	0.5
Kirkcudbright	33 15s	1	18s	0.9	90	0.9	16s	0.8	16s	0.8	16s	0.8	6s	0.3
Wigtown	33 15s	1	15s	0.75	75	0.75	14s	0.7	14s	0.7	8s	0.4	6s	0.3
Whithorn	33 15s	1	5s	0.25	25	0.25	4s	0.2	2s	0.2	2s	0.1	1s	0.05

TABLE I

Tax data for Whithorn and neighbouring burghs (from *Extracts from the Records of the Convention of the Royal Burghs*), demonstrating the low economic status of Whithorn compared with other towns in the area

8s, Whithorn had dropped into the second-lowest group of small burghs alongside places like Annan, Kilrenny or Kintore, and was assessed equally with Stranraer.[198]

In 1692 the burgh's income amounted to about £12 Scots, and its debt was £160. It had no treasurer's books, as its income was so small. The burgesses had a harbour of their own 'if they heade any trade'. Overland trade amounted to 'a small retaill of goods they bring from Air or Dumfriese; the wine, seck, and brandie is soe inconsiderable that they cannot condescend to it'. The burgh did not own or part-own any ships, and many of the houses were ruinous. There were two annual fairs, but no weekly market.[199] Adding to the air of decay was the pitiful condition of the former cathedral. In 1684, when Andrew Symson, minister of Kirkinner, travelled through Galloway and wrote a description of it, he presented a good impression of the cathedral church with its tall western steeple and impressive architectural details.[200] With the overthrow of the Episcopalian regime in 1690, it had again reverted to simple parish status and it appears that there was little expenditure on maintaining its fabric. Early in the eighteenth century the western steeple collapsed, bringing with it the west end of the nave and a substantial portion of the north wall. When repairs were undertaken, the building was patched up on a considerably reduced scale, being shortened in length from the west and lowered in height.[201]

The Isle of Whithorn was the burgh's outport, 'in which ships of a great burthen may be in safety in time of any storme'.[202] In 1655 representatives from Dumfries, Wigtown and Kirkcudbright were to visit the harbour and report to the Convention. In 1660 the town claimed that it needed a 'sufficient harbour', as the present one was 'decayed', and the Convention granted 300 merks towards repairs.[203] In 1677 the Convention recommended voluntary contributions to the harbour of Whithorn, and the following year allowed £10 itself, but in 1680 it was reported that the money had not been spent on the harbour, so the Convention asked for it back.[204]

After 1638, there was little significant building work at the cathedral/parish church until the repair work necessitated by the collapse of the western steeple. Elsewhere in the town, however, there was greater activity, although we know little about the town at this period. There was by then a tolbooth (precise date of construction unknown), which needed repairs in 1664,[205] and in 1692 the hearth tax was paid by 86 households: 59 with one hearth, 22 with two and 5 with three, including the minister and the provost.[206] So although regarding itself as a royal burgh, Whithorn was a small town, with no major houses. If any large houses survived from the medieval period, they were probably by this time either ruinous or subdivided. In the Isle there appears to have been at least some construction work in the late seventeenth century, as indicated by a single surviving datestone of 1674 reused in the outbuildings of the 'castle', but what this work involved is unknown.

The long eighteenth century

One of the great historiographical debates in modern Scottish history has been the question of the state of the national economy in the closing decade of the seventeenth century and opening decade of the eighteenth.[207] Regardless of the health or otherwise of the economy at a national level, in the period c 1690–1740 much of Galloway was experiencing an economic depression. The position in the southern Machars around Whithorn, however, has produced some contradictory evidence which points to a flat economy for much of the eighteenth century but also to early involvement in agricultural improvement and investment in estate development in the neighbourhood of the burgh in the later part of the century.

A continuation of the economic decline which had set in following the Reformation is indicated by a report in 1692 which recorded no foreign trade. This poor situation is perhaps confirmed by Andrew Symson's observation that 'They chose annually a Provest, two Baylies, and a Treasurer (but there is little use for him). Their market-day is Saturday; but it is not at all frequented'.[208] Whithorn, it appears, had no sources of revenue to speak of from either local or foreign trade, common funds, rents or other income. The decades around the turn of the century also comprised a period of regular crop-failures, crises in food supply, and localised famine across Scotland generally, characterised by the 'Seven Ill Years' in the 1690s. At Whithorn, there are indications of a general shortage of particular resources, especially fuel, in this period before the large-scale development of the Ayrshire coalfields. Peat and firewood were increasingly difficult to obtain,[209] while timber for building was also scarce. The general view is that this situation began to improve only in the second half of the eighteenth century. By the late eighteenth century, Galloway, despite its relative isolation from the expanding economic heartland of Scotland and its peripheral geographical location, 'was in the vanguard of agrarian development'. Several of its principal landowners had been leading figures in the agricultural experimentation in the earlier part of the century which saw the rise of what is referred to as the Agricultural Improvement.[210] Their investment and experimentation was occurring at a time when capital was supposedly scarce, the regional economy stagnant, and the spirit of entrepreneurialism suppressed. Mixed agriculture, however, was less susceptible to market fluctuations, and most good land in Galloway was not far from the coast, from which produce could be shipped to neighbouring areas which were more industrial, especially England.[211] The advantages of geography were well recognised in the early nineteenth-century agricultural reports which promoted the further development of Improvement practices: 'The richest lands lie upon the coast; where the means of improvement are to be met with in the greatest abundance'.[212] Most of the produce was exported by sea to England, though cattle were usually driven, mainly to markets in Norfolk and Suffolk.[213] Perhaps because of the accessibility of many small ports, the area had no major fairs which could have served as local economic stimuli.

There may have been hopes for a revival in the local economy earlier in the 1700s during the preliminary moves towards parliamentary union between Scotland and England. The burgh's political life was then dominated by the 5th Earl of Galloway, who was a member of the so-called Court Party in the Scottish parliament and inclined towards the benefits of union. In 1703, the earl arranged for the election of his recently widowed brother-in-law, John Clerk of Penicuik, as MP for the burgh, while Galloway's kinsman, the 2nd Duke of Queensberry, engineered Clerk's rapid rise in the political establishment in Edinburgh. Clerk became one of the Commissioners treating for the union with England, and his detailed knowledge of Scotland's financial state and the condition of the economy was to be a major factor in his role in promoting the Union Bill in the Scottish parliament.[214] The Earl of Galloway (and Whithorn) may have hoped for some economic betterment from union, but the burgh's decline continued into the eighteenth century and showed no significant revival after the Act of Union of 1707 had opened up trade between Scotland and England and given Scottish merchants legal access to the English colonies with which they had already been dealing illicitly for decades. Unfortunately, it was the better-established trading burghs on the west coast, such as Ayr, which benefited most from the development of the Atlantic trade, and Whithorn apparently continued to languish in the economic doldrums.

The continuing poor state of the Scottish economy in the period after the Union was one contributory factor in the upsurge of support for the exiled Stuarts in the early eighteenth century. In Galloway, Jacobite sympathies were confined mainly to some of the leading families in the northern and eastern areas, headed by the Gordons of Lochinvar, Viscounts Kenmure. Although the 6th Viscount Kenmure was a leading figure in the 1715 Jacobite rebellion, raising a small local force and marching into north-western England to join up with the Earl of Derwentwater, only to be defeated and captured by government soldiers at Preston, the main action in the rising bypassed Galloway. Indifference or hostility towards the Jacobite cause in Galloway may have been largely a consequence of the entrenched support within the region for Presbyterianism and strong hostility to the Episcopalianism and Roman Catholicism with which the exiled Stuarts were associated. The failure of the rebellion even to disturb the normal routine of public life in the region is clearly evident in surviving local records. Whithorn kirk session minutes, for example, show no break, unlike kirk session and council minutes in other places in Scotland where the Jacobite cause enjoyed support amongst sections of the burgess and landowning classes.[215] 'Only in the south-western part of Scotland does the Whig interest seem to have enjoyed overwhelming support. Counties like Ayr and Galloway had very old traditions of radical Protestantism which made them highly resistant to Jacobitism'.[216]

While the 1715 rebellion had drawn some support from the great landowning families of eastern Galloway, the forfeiture and execution of the 6th Viscount Kenmure had broken the power of the Jacobite Gordons and removed any pro-Stuart political leadership from the region. Whig and Hanoverian support in Galloway appears to have been pretty well universal after 1715 and there was no significant local sympathy for the Jacobites. The '45 appears to have had no impact at all in terms of support for the rebellion, but the political and legal reforms that were introduced in the wake of its suppression had significant ramifications for local proprietors. One of the most profound consequences was the abolition of heritable jurisdictions in 1747. This, at a stroke, removed the apparatus of private jurisdictional franchises exercised through barony and regality courts, as well as the heritable tenure of legal offices, such as sheriffships. At Whithorn, this legislation affected the regality jurisdiction which had once been exercised by the priors of Whithorn and which had passed into lay hands following the Reformation. The Earl of Galloway, as successor to the prior, was paid £166 compensation for the loss of his rights of regality.[217] After this date the family, although owning property in and around Whithorn,[218] invested money in founding the new town of Garlieston, a rival port to the Isle, thereby further weakening Whithorn's economic prospects.[219]

An agricultural economy

The agricultural improvements which some early eighteenth-century lairds saw as the key to economic revival were not universally popular. Enclosure, as practised on the Earl of Galloway's property, stoked bitter resentment amongst the small tenants who were being squeezed out to make room for larger, consolidated tenancies. Hostility erupted in 1723–24 in the so-called Levellers' rising, protesting at the building of stone dykes to divide up the land. The impact of this resistance appears to have been very variable and localised. While it may have slowed the move towards agricultural improvement in some parts of Galloway, enclosure continued in the Machars and, as improved farming methods were introduced more widely, the numbers needed to work the land were reduced. There were no rapidly growing towns locally to absorb these people, so the eighteenth century saw much emigration. Sources towards the end of the century note that 'The spirit of improvement that at present pervades a great part of Scotland, will, it is to be hoped, soon find its way into Galloway'. The main obstacles were the salt tax, and thirlage,[220] but despite this, 'The face of the country is improving daily, not only by the cultivation bestowed upon the land, but by a passion for planting which shows itself among the landholders'. Farmhouses had 'improved very much within the last twenty years. They are often covered with slate, and divided into convenient apartments. Sheds and straw-yards are coming into general use'.[221] 'Wigton Bay, for many thousand acres, has a rich clay bottom; and the practicability of laying it dry is confidently talked of by people of knowledge in embanking, and has long been a favourite idea of the Earl of Selkirk.'[222] The neighbouring parish of Glasserton exported cattle by land, but sheep and surplus grain by sea to Whitehaven or Liverpool.[223]

A new confidence appeared in the writings of economic commentators and would-be Improvers in the later decades of the eighteenth century. Whithorn and its surrounding district was seen to be particularly well placed to benefit from economic developments, particularly the rapidly growing demand for produce, especially meat, from the expanding urban population in England. 'The advantages of this neighbourhood for trade are obvious. Its grain, and herds of black cattle; its flocks of sheep, with fine wool; its rivulets, and water-carriage to the best markets, all point it out as the seat of commerce.'[224] In the 1790s everyone was grateful for the removal of the tax on coastal shipping of coal, but salt laws were still a burden which hindered the development of trade. Rock-salt from Cheshire was so much better than Scottish salt that it was 'a temptation to smuggling, which cannot be resisted'.[225] It was argued that if the high duties levied on the shipping of salt were removed, some cattle could be salted locally instead of driven south. Droving was wasteful, as the driver charged a tenth of the price at which the beast were sold, and en route they lost about one-eighth of their body-weight; losses due to accidents further reduced the profit margin.[226]

As early as the 1720s, some forward-looking lairds had recognised the advantages to be had by concentrating their efforts on cattle-breeding for the meat trade, but the result by the end of the eighteenth century was a possible over-dependence in the regional economy on agricultural production. Despite some efforts to develop industry in Galloway, most notably at Newton Stewart and Gatehouse of Fleet, the region remained overwhelmingly agricultural, and exposed to all the hazards of such an economic basis. The risks were recognised, one commentator observing that by 1810:

> The chief, and indeed almost the only exports from Galloway consist of
> grain, wool, sheep and black cattle, which are sent … to England, and

to some other parts of Scotland. The imports are lime, coals, wool, all sorts of groceries and manufactured goods, chiefly from England. Wood is sometimes imported directly from America, and both wood and iron from the Baltic. But though attempts have been made to enlarge the commerce of the country by trading to the West Indies, as well as to America and the Baltic on a larger scale; and also to embark in the herring fishery – these attempts have never hitherto been successful.[227]

Dependence on agriculture was reflected in the local position at Whithorn. Bishop Pococke, who visited in 1760, wrote: 'This town consists mostly of farmers and a few tradesmen and manufacturers in woollen and linen for home consumption'.[228] While the parish may have seen agricultural improvement for the best part of half a century by Pococke's day, there was no indication of Whithorn deriving benefit, but by the 1790s that position had evidently changed. Although the New Galloway-born writer Robert Heron (1764–1807) described Whithorn as 'an inconsiderable burgh, infamous as the haunt of smugglers', smuggling being common during much of the eighteenth century, he added that 'some years ago, a spirit for trade began to show itself'.[229] This 'spirit for trade' may have been responsible for the beginnings of an expansion of the burgh beyond the medieval limits which had defined it since its establishment in the fourteenth century.

Manufacturing

What the 'spirit for trade' involved at Whithorn is unclear, for there is no substantial evidence for involvement in manufacturing, although the rate of agricultural improvement does appear to have accelerated in the closing decades of the eighteenth century. Galloway, like much of rural Scotland, participated in the early phases of the industrial revolution, but lost out when steam power led to the concentration of resources in large conurbations with plenty of labour and good transport networks. There was an established tradition of woollen-textile production in Galloway generally, and records of a waulkmill for the finishing of woollen cloth at Pouton (Poltoun), owned by the priory, together with the references to a trade in woollens in the late fifteenth and sixteenth centuries, point to Whithorn's early involvement in manufacture and export.[230] The lack of a suitable watercourse from which to power one of the new, mechanised manufactories which were being constructed in the later eighteenth century, however, probably ensured that Whithorn missed out on the development of an industrialised cloth-production operation. Ian Donnachie has suggested that woollens were 'probably the first manufacturing industry to be revitalised by capital investment'. Several water-powered mills were built elsewhere in Galloway after the 1770s, mostly by local entrepreneurs or merchants, but these were involved principally in the processing of imported cotton rather than local wool or flax for linen. 'The linen industry was never of any great importance in Galloway … The cotton industry was of more lasting importance than linen'.[231] The late 1780s saw the 'cotton-spinning mania', with major mills leading to the growth or even new creation of villages at Newton Douglas, Castle Douglas, and Gatehouse of Fleet, but the boom was short-lived, disrupted by the Napoleonic Wars. 'Previous to the commencement of the present war, near 600 hands might be employed in the different manufactures, of which the cotton spinning at Gate-House was by far the most extensive. Since that period, the number has daily been on the decline'.[232] The cotton mills at Gatehouse and Newton Stewart failed despite good water power and good roads offering access to markets.[233]

Access to capital for investment appears to have been difficult and may have been a major factor in limiting local entrepreneurs. Something of a vicious circle may have resulted, for the absence of economic growth in the area occasioned by a lack of investment may have deterred would-be investors from speculating in the region. One key manifestation of this can be seen in the under-provision of banking facilities in south-western Scotland. There had been some early moves to rectify this situation with the establishment in 1769 of the Ayr Bank (Douglas, Heron & Co), with a branch in Dumfries. Its collapse in 1772 may have had long-term consequences, for it was said to have 'dampened spirits' and inhibited agricultural improvements.[234] The first bank in Galloway was the Bank of Scotland, which opened a branch in Wigtown in 1784, followed by one in Kirkcudbright in 1789–90. A branch of the British Linen Bank was opened in Wigtown in 1785, but moved to Newton Stewart in 1801. A branch of Douglas, Heron & Co opened in Castle Douglas in 1806. Apart from these, the nearest banks were in Dumfries, which had a branch of the British Linen Company from 1771, and the Bank of Scotland from 1774.[235] The absence of a bank branch in Whithorn points to the comparative insignificance of the burgh as a commercial or manufacturing centre. The major local proprietors clearly were content to bank in Wigtown.

Although there is physical evidence for the expansion of Whithorn in the years to either side of 1800, it was still apparently not regarded as a significant regional centre. By the 1790s the principal towns in the shire were given as Wigtown, Newton Stewart, Garlieston, Isle of Whithorn, Stranraer and Portpatrick. The recent foundation of Garlieston was clearly regarded as a success, but it was also observed that 'The want of sufficient population, which has retarded improvements in agriculture, operates more powerfully as a bar to the progress of manufactures' in the region generally.[236] Garlieston's success may have been in drawing inhabitants from already established centres in Galloway rather than in attracting colonists from outside the region. The limited development of a manufacturing base continued to be remarked upon. In the parish of Whithorn in the 1790s, the minister noted that tanning was carried out, using hides imported from Ireland rather than from local cattle, and reported that 'Several cotton manufactures have commenced'.[237]

There was also apparently a small distillery, at Smallhill.[238] Agricultural expansion might be indicated by the proliferation of mills, chiefly for grain, but this may also reflect the provision of more convenient mills following the abolition of thirlage. In the 1790s there were five corn mills, four driven by water and one by wind. A windmill on the east side of Isle Street, at the south end of Whithorn, is shown on Roy's map of *c* 1750 (**map 3**), and in a print of *c* 1825, complete with sails.[239] In the mid-nineteenth century it went out of use, was reduced in height and converted into a house, with a spiral outside stair (**fig 24**). Its stump was demolished in the 1960s.[240] Watermills were sited at Portyerrock and the Isle. The latter is probably the Bysbie mill, mentioned in 1545, and shown as such on a map of 1818 (**map 6**).[241]

Roads and harbours

Poor landward communications may have been a further bar to commercial development. The regional road system up to the 1700s appears to have followed the lines established in the Middle Ages and depended on ferries or old, narrow bridges to cross the principal watercourses. The eighteenth century saw radical changes with the construction of military roads, a development driven by the fact that 'Galloway shared with the Highlands an impenetrability which alarmed the military mind of the Hanoverians. The fact that this wild and inhospitable countryside had to be traversed to reach Ireland was an additional incentive to the strategists to press forward

MAP 3
Whithorn; detail from Roy map *c* 1750 (reproduced by permission of the Trustees of the British Library)

FIGURE 24
Windmill on the east side of Isle Street, *c* 1900 (Whithorn Photographic Group. Licensor www.scran.ac.uk)

the improvement of communications'.[242] Built 'to open a speedy, and certain communication between Great Britain and Ireland; especially with regard to the passage of the Troops from one Kingdom to the other, whenever the Exigency of Affairs may require it',[243] the military road ran 'from Bridge of Sark, near Gretna Green, to Port Patrick, with a northern arm from Stranraer to Ballantrae'.[244] There was already some sort of road along this route, but it underwent a major reconstruction, mainly between 1763 and 1765 by Major Rickson, under the overall supervision of Major Caulfield.[245] The provision of this main east–west artery, reinforced in 1796 when the area's first Turnpike Act led to the construction of a road from Dumfries to Castle Douglas, saw the further marginalising of the communities which lay at a distance from the new roads. The Machars, and especially Whithorn, derived little benefit from a roadway which directed traffic towards rival ports in west Wigtownshire, and this situation became entrenched in the following 20 to 30 years with the construction of other new roads, including that from Newton Stewart to Portpatrick, which formed the basis for the modern road network.[246]

Government investment in the new roads led to the development of harbour facilities at Portpatrick and Stranraer, while improvement of the harbour at the Isle fell largely onto the shoulders of local proprietors. In 1745 it was said that the condition of Whithorn had been 'described in one line by a former Provost, "They had a good harbour if they had trade for it"'.[247] This 'good harbour' appears already to have possessed a stone-built pier, which is marked on Roy's map of the early 1750s (**map 4**) and was described in 1760

MAP 4
Isle of Whithorn; detail
from Roy map *c* 1750
(reproduced by permission
of the Trustees of the British
Library)

by Bishop Pococke who noted 'a little harbour formed by a pier, within which they have 18 feet [of] water at high tydes, and a ship of 300 tuns can come in. They export barley, and import plank and iron from Gottenburgh in Sweden, and send it by boats to Wigtown, as the entrance and harbour there are not good'.[248] Sea-borne trade was certainly not thriving in the mid-1700s, but by the 1790s the position had improved substantially. The *Statistical Account* reported that 'From this port vessels sail to Whitehaven and Workington in four hours; to the Isle of Man in three; to Dublin, Greenock and Liverpool in eighteen'.[249]

The facilities then consisted of 'a good natural harbour, improved by a quay. It is narrow at the entrance, but very safe for vessels when in'. 'Eight or nine small sloops belong to this place, in which about 30 mariners are employed. They bring coal and lime from England; carry sea shells from the river Cree, and take away the grain, potatoes, with some fat cattle, sheep, and swine to the different markets.' A new pier was built *c* 1790, with financial help from the Convention of Royal Burghs, and can be seen on a chart of 1793.[250] During the eighteenth century the harbour at the Isle was the base for a Revenue Cutter, part of the Customs service, which operated using both sailing and shore-based officers.[251] At the end of the eighteenth century the 'castle' became the headquarters for the Revenue Protection Service.[252] Fishing boats do not seem to have been permitted to operate from the harbour, indeed, there is little evidence for the development of a significant fishing operation in the parish before the nineteenth century.[253] A chart of 1818 (**map 6**) marks a 'Stone Dyke for intercepting Fish' on the western side of the harbour, consisting of an L-shaped wall located at the lower end of the tidal reach. Although it was presumably in use at the time of the chart's preparation, there is no indication of when it was first constructed.[254]

Whithorn

The physical development of the burgh in the eighteenth century appears to reflect the general economic stagnation of the early 1700s, followed by quite dynamic growth at the end of the century. The most substantial building work in the early part of the century was at the parish church, driven by necessity rather than by any desire to display the community's wealth. The church in the early eighteenth century still occupied the former nave of the medieval priory as refurbished by the seventeenth-century bishops, although stripped of the fittings and trappings of Episcopacy after 1688.[255] In the early eighteenth century the western tower fell, bringing much of the west wall with it. When the wall was rebuilt, internal galleries were added at the east and west ends to accommodate the numbers of parishioners attending services. Where this pressure of numbers was coming from, however, is not altogether clear, for the burgh population does not appear to have grown in the late seventeenth or early eighteenth century, and the policy of enclosure being pursued by the Murrays and the Earl of Galloway may have led to rural depopulation in the landward parts of the parish. In the 1790s, the minister described his church as 'commodious', and the manse, in what was probably the former commendator's house, as 'a good useful house' to which a glebe of seven acres of very good land was attached.[256] The parish church was the only religious building in the town until a Secession (Relief) Church was built in 1793 in St John Street to accommodate a dissenting congregation.[257] It was noted in the *Statistical Account*, however, that there were 'only a few sectaries of the Cameronian and antiburgher descriptions'.[258]

The poor condition of the public buildings in the burgh in the early eighteenth century, which a series of grants from central sources was intended to remedy, possibly reflects the overall weak state of Whithorn's finances at this time. In 1708 the town was granted £5 sterling by the Convention of Royal Burghs towards the rebuilding of its tolbooth, and in 1709 £100 Scots for both tolbooth and harbour.[259] In 1709 it also received 100 merks from the Exchequer towards the building of a steeple and casting of a bell.[260] At the time of Bishop Pococke's visit in 1760, the tolbooth consisted of 'a square tower in the middle of the street, which they always keep well whitened'.[261] It was replaced by a new town house in 1814 (**figs 25 & 26**). There have been suggestions that the present tower may date from the early eighteenth-century rebuilding, but it cannot, as it definitely stands on a different site.[262] A Dutch bell dated 1708 hung in the present steeple, and a stone dated 1709 is built into the rear wall of the present building.[263] The bell is presumably that paid for with Exchequer funds and the date-stone records the rebuilding work undertaken on the old tolbooth at that time.

FIGURE 25
The very domestic George Street frontage of the 1814 town house (Paula Martin)

FIGURE 26
The tolbooth tower behind the 1814 town house, seen from the priory (Colin Martin)

A generally favourable picture of the burgh's condition is offered in descriptive accounts of the mid- and late eighteenth century. In 1745 the town was described as having 'a tolbooth, a cross, a pillory, and a most insecure prison, two stout gates, at the High Port and Laigh Port, and about 1000 inhabitants'.[264] Half a century later, it was reported that

> The town consists chiefly of one street, running from N. to S. From this street there are several alleys stretching to the E. and to the W. About the centre of the town, there is a good hall for public meetings, adorned with a spire and turrets, and provided with a set of bells. A beautiful stream of water, over which there is a good bridge, runs across the main street, dividing it nearly into two equal parts. The houses are generally covered with slates, and made very commodious.[265]

Another writer, perhaps paraphrasing the above account, reported that 'the houses are tolerably well built'.[266]

Isle of Whithorn and Garlieston

In 1760 the village of Isle of Whithorn was described thus: 'The principal houses are on the west side of it, and on the Isle near the bridge is a row of poor houses. This part of the isle is flat, and in high seas the water seems to have come over and divided it from the rising ground beyond it'.[267] Roy's map of c 1750 (**map 4**) and Ainslie's of 1782 show the Isle before the causeway was built up. The castle stands by the millpond, and houses cluster around both road junctions. Better, more detailed plans survive for the Isle than for Whithorn itself. One dated 1780 (**map 5**) shows the castle, mill, millpond and mill-lade, with a few houses to the west and slightly more to the east, but no indication of whether there were others beyond the edges of the plan.[268] A chart of the harbour drawn in 1818 (**map 6**) shows elevations of the buildings surrounding the harbour.[269] Most are of two storeys, and in much the same positions as today. The houses on the quayside are single storey. The surviving warehouses must, in their present form therefore, post-date 1818 (**fig 27**), but 'storehouses' are on record from 1795, and the line of buildings is shown on Roy's map of c 1750 (**map 4**).[270]

In 1777 Whithorn council was in dispute with the new village and harbour of Garlieston, which it saw as encroaching on its traditional rights. Garlieston had been founded c 1760 by John, 7th Earl of Galloway, then Lord Garlies, on the west shore of Garlieston Bay, north of Galloway House. Situated in the adjacent parish of Sorbie, Garlieston was only five miles from Whithorn. Established at a time of expanding coastal shipping, it had the potential to become a serious rival to Isle of Whithorn, from whose harbour Whithorn derived the bulk of its revenue, 'having little else than what they collect by way of shore dues and anchorages within the limits of their grants, which they annually let to a tacksman'.[271] The threat from Garlieston was

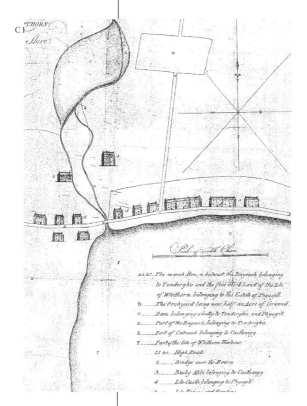

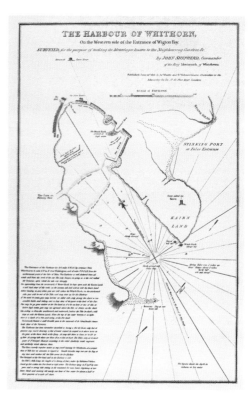

MAP 5

NAS RHP663, 'Sketch of the Orchard etc. of Isle of Whithorn in Galloway Shire', 1780 (reproduced by permission of the Trustees of the National Archives of Scotland)

MAP 6

NAS RHP 42253, detail from Admiralty Chart of 'The Harbour of Whithorn ... surveyed ... by John Shepherd, Commander of the Brig *Monmouth* of Whitehaven', 1818 (reproduced by permission of the Trustees of the National Archives of Scotland)

FIGURE 27

Nineteenth-century warehouses on the pier at Isle of Whithorn photographed in the 1970s. They have since been converted (see **fig 54**) (Crown copyright: Historic Scotland)

complicated by the influence of the Stewarts of Galloway in Wigtownshire politics: during the eighteenth century, the parliamentary votes for Whithorn and Wigtown were controlled by the earls of Galloway.

Old Statistical Account: comparisons and occupations

By the end of the eighteenth century Whithorn appears to have regained a measure of prosperity, perhaps associated with the economic restructuring which had arisen from local agricultural improvement. Although it is recorded that in 1774 a few people had emigrated to America 'to bemoan their folly in uncultivated deserts',[272] population levels appear to have been quite stable. The *Statistical Account* of 1794 presents a record of a minor provincial burgh with an economy integrated closely with that of its rural and coastal hinterland. Whithorn then had a population of 756, making it the 140th largest town in Scotland. Comparison with the other main towns in the county, however, show how its position had slipped, only in relation to its old local rival, Wigtown, but to the newer developments which had prospered due to their location on the main road networks. Stranraer, with 1602 inhabitants, was the 61st largest community in Scotland and already more than double the size of Whithorn, while Newton Stewart, with 1100 inhabitants, held 97th place and Wigtown's 1032 inhabitants put it in 105th place.[273]

The inhabitants of the parish of Whithorn in 1794 included 1 clergyman, 1 writer, 1 attorney, 1 plasterer, 1 saddler, 18 masons and 1 apprentice, 16 joiners and 11 apprentices, 2 slaters, 25 weavers and 2 apprentices, 22 shoemakers and 2 apprentices, 16 tailors and 2 apprentices, 8 blacksmiths and 1 apprentice, 2 customs officers, 12 shopkeepers, 2 coopers and 1 apprentice. It is a profile which suggests a small craft- and trades-based community serving the needs of the rural population. There were four inns and twelve ale or whisky

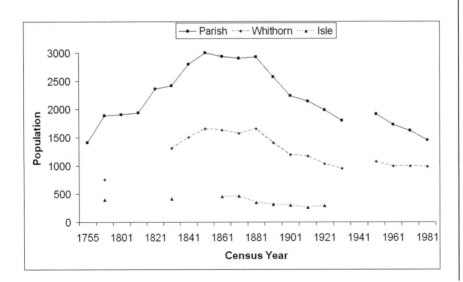

TABLE 2
Population figures for Whithorn parish, Whithorn burgh and Isle of Whithorn

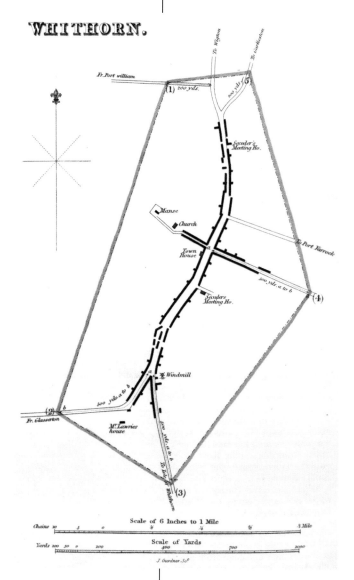

WHITHORN.

Scale of 6 Inches to 1 Mile

Scale of Yards

J. Gardner Sc.t

MAP 7
Parliamentary boundary
map, 1832 (from *Report
upon the boundaries of the
several cities burghs and
towns of Scotland … 1832*)

houses in the parish.[274] Social activities for the wealthier burgesses and local lairds do not seem to have been well provided for, but by 1801 there was a masonic lodge in the town, St Thomas.[275] Another list from 1798–99, for the burgh only, included 7 wrights, 5 cotton-spinners, 4 merchants, 4 masons, 3 shoemakers, 3 tailors, 3 smiths, 3 weavers, 1 flesher and 1 tanner.[276] A significant rise in population began in the years after *c* 1790 (**table 2**), triggered by an increase in immigrants from Ireland, both Protestant and Catholic, especially to Newton Stewart, Whithorn and Stranraer. This influx may account for a significant portion of the increase in population, and is perhaps to be seen most clearly in the almost doubling of the footprint of the burgh between the plan produced by Roy in the 1750s and the parliamentary boundary map of 1832 (**map 7**).

c 1820–1914

Introduction

For Whithorn, the century preceding the outbreak of the First World War appears to have seen the peak of its post-medieval prosperity followed by a long, slow decline. The 'boom and bust' seems to have stemmed mainly from its overwhelming dependence on the agricultural productivity of its rural hinterland. This resulted in a heavy exposure to the consequences of the prolonged periods of depression in the agricultural economy which punctuated the nineteenth century. Economic migration, mainly of agricultural labourers, appears to have produced a significant increase in population levels in the southern Machars in the early nineteenth century (see **table 2**), in contrast with the later eighteenth century which saw a substantial reduction in the labour force. Settlement was perhaps encouraged by the efforts of improving landlords to develop their properties.[277] Whithorn benefited from both an increase in its resident population and a general stimulation to its economy as the value of the agricultural products increased. Unfortunately, however, there was no parallel development of a manufacturing base, with the consequence that every shift in the fortunes of the agricultural economy had an almost immediate impact on Whithorn.

Administrative structure of the burgh

Throughout this period of challenge, the administrative structure of the burgh remained largely unchanged. The town was governed by a provost, 2 bailies, a treasurer, 6 councillors, and from 1832 until 1885 it joined with Wigtown, New Galloway, Newton Stewart and Stranraer (Wigtown District of Burghs) to elect an MP. The first significant change came in 1873 when the town adopted most sections of the General Police and Improvement (Scotland) Act of 1862. Accordingly, members of the town council became police commissioners, responsible for cleansing, lighting, policing and public health. The Town Councils (Scotland) Act of 1901 formally replaced police commissioners by town councillors. The actual impact which these structural changes had is questionable, given the slender revenues available to the council, and the economic peaks and troughs of the period can be seen to have had a direct impact upon the effectiveness of its operations.

The economy

Despite the apparent evidence for an improvement in the economy of Whithorn in the later eighteenth and early nineteenth century, in 1825 the town was described as 'formerly a place of commercial importance; but at present the trade is very inconsiderable'.[278] The parliamentary boundaries report of 1832 was similarly dismissive: 'It consists almost entirely of one Street. It has no trade or manufactures, and there is no prospect of increase'.[279] In the industrialisation of Scotland of the early nineteenth century and the development of the first global market for produce, Whithorn was falling further and further behind. Despite the continuing programmes of agricultural improvement, Galloway's regional economy remained significantly poorer than that of central or eastern Scotland through its overwhelming dependence on agricultural production.[280] Certainly there was a growing market for that produce as Britain's urban labouring population boomed, but the poor state of the communications network in southern Wigtownshire perhaps hindered the district's fuller integration into that market.

The agricultural nature of the town's hinterland and the relative absence of easily exploitable non-agricultural resources, such as coal or mineral ores, coupled with the poor transportation system which hindered both the import of raw materials for manufacturing and the export of finished articles, ensured that there was to be no industrial expansion of Whithorn as the century progressed.[281] The overwhelmingly agricultural nature of the community and the resources available locally is reflected in a Directory of 1825 which lists two tanners, a grazier, a saddler, and a tallow-chandler.[282] The primary emphasis of the agricultural improvement movement in the district appears to have been on improving the quality of pasture and developing a cattle-based economy, although there was also significant development of barley production where the ground suited it. By the 1830s more cattle were being retained locally and fattened up, instead of being driven to distant markets, and some were shipped to Liverpool. The investment in new farm buildings, which may have been responsible for the noticeable strength of the building trade in Whithorn at the end of the eighteenth century, continued through the second decade of the nineteenth century. 'Good dwelling houses and office houses upon farms add much to the appearance of a country; and sure no set of men deserve good lodgings more than farmers do. In this parish these have improved very much within the last 20 years. They are often covered with slate and divide into convenient apartments'.[283] Mill buildings, too, appear to have been undergoing redevelopment at this time and each of the three main burns in the parish 'turns a corn and barley-mill, where it falls into the sea'. The surviving buildings at the Isle and Portyerrock appear to be of nineteenth-century date. The burgh's principal grain mill, however, appears to have been the windmill at the top of the town which was in operation by the eighteenth century.[284] Water supply was not, apparently, an issue, for there were also 'perennial limpid rills', providing abundant water for people and cattle,[285] and for associated 'industrial' processes, especially tanning, but not with an adequate fall for a waterwheel. There was, for example, a tannery on the Ket south-east of the main street.[286]

While Whithorn was clearly a service centre for its rural hinterland, it remained also the primary market centre for the southern Machars, with a weekly market on Thursdays.[287] Two fairs had traditionally been held, at Midsummer and Lammas, and a monthly cattle market between April and January, but by the 1870s only the Midsummer fair was being held, in July. This fair was of declining importance and by the 1890s was remembered as having once been 'the greatest annual concourse ... in Western Galloway'.[288] These were all minor affairs, however, and 'The local trade is very inconsiderable, and merely of a retail and domestic character'.[289] Any hope that the cattle market would acquire a regional significance based on the development of pastoral farming in the southern Machars and sea-borne trade from the Isle or Garlieston had been unfulfilled.

The balance of occupations within Whithorn changed hardly at all over the period.[290] By the 1890s Wigtownshire was 'almost exclusively an agricultural and grazing county, its manufactures, commerce and mining being of little importance'.[291] The emphasis within agriculture, however, continued to change as market demand and the communications infrastructure altered. The principal change was the coming of the railways, which put an end to the droving of cattle. This was followed by a gradual change towards more cattle being kept for the production of milk than for beef.

Banking and finance

Scotland's developing financial sector resulted in a steady increase in the provision of regional and local banking services during the second quarter of the nineteenth century. There was now apparently sufficient business in the southern Machars for branch offices in the town to be viable. The first bank in Whithorn was the Edinburgh and Glasgow Bank, which set up at no. 79 George Street (**fig 12**), some time between 1837 and 1849.[292] A second door and pillars were added to the existing building. In 1858 the Edinburgh and Glasgow was taken over by the Clydesdale, which in the 1870s moved to new premises next door, at no. 77 George Street.[293] The Edinburgh and Glasgow was joined by 1849 by the National Bank, which in 1886 moved to the premises at nos 19/21 George Street which are still occupied by its successor, the Royal Bank of Scotland.[294] A savings bank had been established in *c* 1810, and by 1839 had an operating capital of around £2500. There were also two friendly societies, but these had been wound up by 1839.[295] For such a small community, the provision of two commercial banks and one savings bank is indicative of a level of economic activity at variance with other sources of evidence, suggesting perhaps the patronage of these banks by some of the larger farmers and landowners in the neighbourhood.

Whithorn Burgh as a corporate entity does not appear to have been a potential client for these banks. In the absence of any significant property from which a common fund could be built, the main source of income was harbour dues from Isle of Whithorn, which 'conducts some commerce with Whitehaven and other English ports, having a well-sheltered harbour … with capacity and external advantages sufficient to invite extensive commerce'.[296] Trade through the Isle was relatively high during the mid-nineteenth century, principally as a result of the development of the steamer traffic. This development of steam shipping and more regular services from the harbours of Galloway to north-western England began to open up wider markets for cattle and other produce. Consequently, agriculture became more profitable. It was later claimed that trade had been 'very considerable', but after the coming of the railway had 'greatly diminished'.[297] This is borne out by published figures: in 1839 it was reported that 'The burgh has a small revenue … arising from harbour-dues and fees', [298] In 1831 the burgh's total revenue had been £153 8s, made up of £119 (78%) from harbour dues, £14 8s from kirk seat rents, one croft yielding £5, feu duties amounting to £5, £3 10s rent for the windmill, and a few other oddments. It had risen to £230 11s by 1840 with the start of steamer traffic. In 1874 it was much the same, at £228, but had dropped sharply to £80 by 1884, and by 1895 was only £36.[299] These figures correspond with the population figures (**table 2**), with the number of inhabitants in 1841 almost double that of 1794, and remaining at around that level until 1881, after which it started to decline. The decrease in the burgh's income coincides with the arrival in 1877 of the railway from Wigtown and Newton Stewart.

Directories	1825	1837	1852	1867	1873	1878	1882	1886	1889	1893	1900	1903	1907	1911	1915
Whithorn															
Population		1305	1652	1632	1577	1577	1651	1653	1653	1403	1403	1188	1188	1170	1170
Resident gentry	1	5	14	12	10	13	17	19		14	13	10	16	17	16
Writers	1	2	2	1	1	2	2	1	3	2	2	3	3	3	3
Doctors (1 physician 1825, rest surgeons)	4	3	3	4	3	2	2	2	2	2	2	2	2	2	2
Banks (Clydesdale & National)	x	x	2	2	2	2	2	2	2	2	2	2	2	2	1
Hotels	x	x	a	2	2	2	2	2	2	2	2	2	3	3	3
Galloway Arms				y	y	y	y	y	y	y	y	y	y	y	y
Grapes		y	y	y	y	y	y	y	y	y	y	y	y	y	y
Temperance													y	y	y
Innkeepers/vintners	8	15	8	5	5	7	5	5	5	5	5	4	4	4	5
Brunswick				y	y	y	y	y	y	y	y	y	y	y	y
Calcutta (St Jn St)							y	y	y	y	y	y	y	y	y
Commercial		y	y	y	y	y	y	y	y	y	y	y	y	y	y
King's Arms (1825)/Head	y		y												
Plough				y											
Red Lion				y											
Masons & wrights, builders	x	3	9	8	9	8	11	9	9	12	6	5	7	5	4
Isle of Whithorn															
Population		413		458	459	459	353	352	352	316	316	301	301	261	261
Resident gentry	2	1	1	8	7	5	5	5		3	3	4	2	5	6
Vinterns/innkeepers	6	5	4	2	2	2	2	2	2	2	2	2	2	2	2
Queen's Arms				y	y	y	y	y	y	y	y	y	y	y	y
Steam Packet				y	y	y	y	y	y	y	y	y	y	y	y
Shipwrights	x	2	2	1	1	1	1	1	1	x	x	x	x	x	x
Merchants (coal, grain, lime etc)	x	x	x	1	1	2	3	3	3	2	1	1	1	1	1
Miller (+ Port Yarrock to 1893 or later)	x	1	1	1	1	1	1	1	1	1	1	1	1	1	1
Master mariners			3						1	1					
Salmon fisher				1											

TABLE 3
Occupational and other information from Trade Directories between 1825 and 1915 (from *Pigot's* and *Slater's Directories*)

The town continued to function, 'almost entirely due to the central situation which it occupies in a rich agricultural district',[300] but in 1888 the town council was bankrupt. As a consequence, the Isle of Whithorn Harbour Company was established to manage the harbour.[301] The general flatness of the economic condition of Whithorn contrasts sharply with evidence for much greater activity at the Isle through the same period, as indicated by trades directories (**table 3**). Shipwrights are listed between 1837 and 1889, and merchants from 1867, dealing in the cargoes imported or exported there, including coal, grain and lime. Although there was little fishing, 'around 1880 a fleet of oyster fishing boats from England operated off the coast, storing their catches in a marine pond at the Blue Hole'.[302] The watermill at Portyerrock went out of use around the end of the century but Bysbie mill at the Isle was working into the twentieth century.[303]

Port and rail links

Land and sea communications through the Isle developed significantly in the second quarter of the nineteenth century. In the1830s public roads ran from Whithorn and Garlieston to the Isle, and from Whithorn to Port William and Stranraer, and a mail coach was crossing the parish each day.[304] The New Statistical Account of 1839 noted that 'small vessels sail every week [from the Isle] to Whitehaven and other English ports', and it was 'occasionally visited by the Galloway steamer on her way to and from Liverpool'.[305] 'The passage of large herds of Irish cattle and of much British merchandise, together with the presence of numerous travellers, conferred a considerable local benefit, which, however, has now almost entirely been diverted by the development of steam navigation'.[306] Steam shipping, which had once seemed to be a potential saviour, offering faster and safer services for the export of produce by sea, was in the longer term to weaken the area's links with England and Ireland, and increase links with the rest of Scotland.[307] Instead of short coastal or cross-Solway hops in small vessels, dependent very much on wind direction and strength, which had also made the Isle a port of refuge on a very exposed coast, the larger cargo-carrying steamers made longer voyages, were independent of the vagaries of the wind, and could carry in one load what previously had needed several vessels or trips to transport. The nature of the harbour itself was a major deterrent to further development, as it was unable to accommodate the vessels of deeper draught and longer keels which were becoming more common. Yet in 1900 there was a fortnightly steamer service from the Isle to Glasgow.

The entrance to the port was difficult because of rocks and a tide-race, and the pier suffered from storm damage, but the row of warehouses on the pier testifies to the importance of sea-borne trade during this period. Shipbuilding is said to have begun c 1799, and ended in the 1860s, though ship repairs continued, as there was at least one shipwright on the Isle until c 1890 (**table 3**).[308] However, shipbuilding was also under way at nearby Garlieston by the 1830s.[309] In 1906 the harbour at Isle of Whithorn was described thus: 'The pier … admits vessels drawing eight or nine feet of water inside it at half tide, and at the pierhead those of eighteen feet draught on springs and thirteen on neaps … there is a patent slip adapted for vessels of 550 tons. A few vessels are built and repaired'.[310] 'Trading vessels were built and launched near the Old Ha' and also at the Black Rocks'.[311]

The Revenue presence continued (see p 64). In 1852 the local Customs service had its base at Wigtown, with coast-officers at Creetown, Garlieston, Gatehouse, Isle of Whithorn and Portwilliam. In 1832 some of the shore-based activities of the Customs service were moved to a separate but subordinate organisation, the Coastguard, from 1856 part of the Admiralty. Coastguards were active in attempts to reduce smuggling, as well as dealing with any shipwrecks, and one of their bases was at the Isle. The small tower on the highest part of the promontory was a daymark built to support a flagstaff and act as a visual aid for ships making for the harbour. This exposed spot was formerly the coastguard station, and there remain on the rocks traces of rings for erecting a tent to shelter the men in their watch in wild weather, and a carved compass rose.[312] In 1868 a stone lifeboat house was built on the neck of land between the chapel and the daymark, so that the boat could be launched and rowed in either direction. The new lifeboat started work in 1869.[313]

The development which made the greatest impact was the arrival of the railway. A line, mainly locally financed, had been built in 1859 from Dumfries to Castle Douglas, and continued to Portpatrick two years later, with branch lines from Castle Douglas to Stranraer completed in 1863, and to Kirkcudbright in 1864. In 1871 a public meeting was held in Newton Stewart to discuss building a line to Whithorn. Under the leadership of Lord Garlies, heir to the Earl of Galloway, the Wigtownshire Railway Company was formed. Although not all the shares had been sold, it was agreed to begin work on the first section, which was easier in engineering terms, and in 1875 the line was opened to Wigtown. The following year the Bladnoch was crossed by a viaduct, the short branch to Garlieston was completed, and the railway continued towards Whithorn. There was a risk that the money would run out before the last section could be built, but the Earl of Galloway led the raising of extra subscriptions and the railway reached Whithorn in 1877.[314] The last line to be built in Galloway, the Wigtownshire Railway 'presents a particularly interesting example of a branch line constructed and operated almost entirely on local capital and initiative' and a 'case-study of the effects of railway development in an isolated agricultural district, which traditionally relied on sea links'.[315] Its construction was an act of optimism and the line was always barely profitable; in 1885 the company merged with the Portpatrick Railway and operations were taken over by the Glasgow and South-Western Railway.

The primary aim behind the development of the railway was the potential benefits it would bring to the local economy. Certainly, the rail link helped in exporting agricultural produce, but it killed off the shipping of cattle to Liverpool, thereby driving down income from harbour dues at the Isle. The station and yards stood at the north end of the town, and may have served as a focus for further development, such as the creamery, whose produce could be transported by rail. There were also hopes that the railway would bring in tourists: as late as the 1950s Whithorn was being promoted as the 'southernmost terminus in Scotland'.[316]

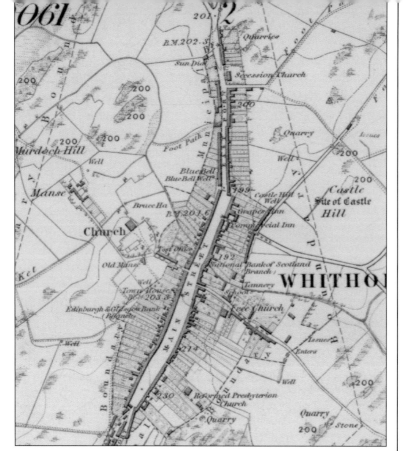

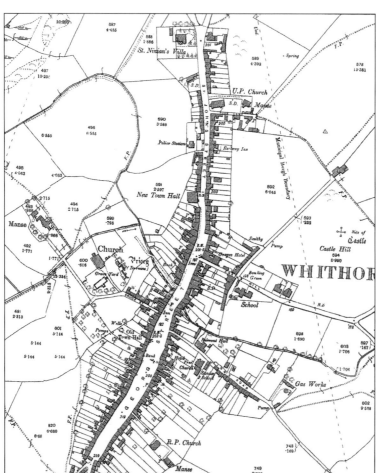

MAP 8
a) First edition OS 6" map
of Whithorn, surveyed 1849
(reproduced by permission
of the Trustees of the
National Library of Scotland)
b) First edition OS 1:2500
map of Whithorn, surveyed
1894/5 (reproduced by
permission of the Trustees
of the National Library of
Scotland)

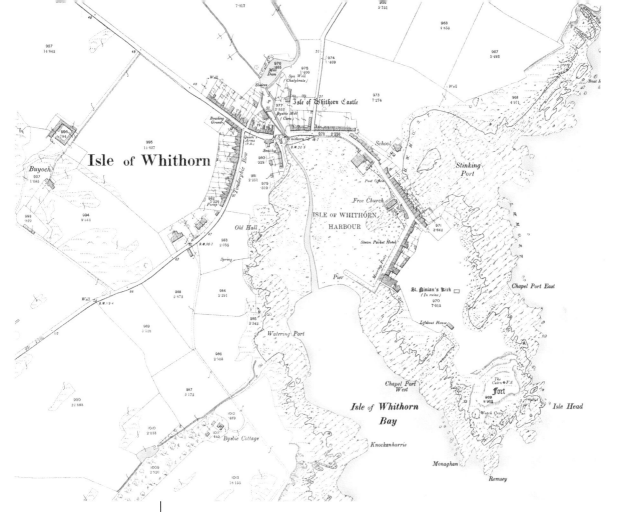

MAP 9
a) First edition OS 1:2500 map of Isle of Whithorn, surveyed 1895 (reproduced by permission of the Trustees of the National Library of Scotland)
b) First edition OS 6" map of Isle of Whithorn, surveyed 1849 (reproduced by permission of the Trustees of the National Library of Scotland)

Tourism

Tourism had made a limited impact in Galloway generally in the later eighteenth and early nineteenth century. With the exception of Bishop Pococke, none of the best-known travellers who published descriptions of their trips in Scotland, such as Thomas Pennant, the Wordsworths or Coleridge, visited the area. Sir Walter Scott's novels had stimulated tourist traffic to the Highlands, the Trossachs and the eastern Borders in the 1830s, but, despite the success of his book *Redgauntlet* (or *The Bride of Lammermuir*), large parts of which were set in the south-west, there was no similar interest generated in visiting Galloway. What 'tourism' there was appears to have been very limited and local. In 1839 the minister had noted that 'There is a weak chalybeate spring at the Isle of Whithorn, occasionally resorted to by invalids'.[317] Gradually, however, as the use of the harbour declined in the later nineteenth century, and passenger transport improved, small-scale tourism began to develop. 'The district', commented one local writer, 'has remained unknown to the world longer than any part of Scotland with the possible exception of the island of Rockall'.[318] By the turn of the century the Isle was beginning to attract a small but wealthy clientele seeking sea air; in 1911 there were apartments available at the Castle and Boston Cottage, and one boarding house.[319]

The provision of accommodation remained limited, however, and was mostly designed to cater for commercial travellers. The volume of accommodation did increase after the arrival of the railway in 1877, some of it intended to capitalise on increased visitor numbers. For most of the nineteenth century there were two hotels in Whithorn: the Grapes and the

FIGURE 28
The post office, formerly the Galloway Arms, another building with exposed multi-coloured greywacke and painted margins
(Paula Martin)

Galloway Arms (now the post office) (**fig 28**). These were joined by 1907 by a Temperance Hotel nearer the station (now the Black Hawk). There were also five inns, including the Brunswick (now the Central Café, no. 17 George Street), the Commercial Inn (originally at the junction of Castlehill and George Street, but moved in the 1930s to near the Pend), the King's Head, the 'once celebrated hostelry' called the Red Lion, and, from *c* 1880, the Calcutta in High Street (see **fig 41**). In the Isle were the Steam Packet and the Queen's Arms.[320] The agricultural nature of the district and the absence of major Victorian and Edwardian tourist draws such as shooting and fishing, golf and other outdoor pursuits ensured, however, that visitor numbers remained low and the scale of hotel accommodation reflects this position.

Churches

Few public buildings were erected in Whithorn during the nineteenth century, the largest single development being a new parish church, with 800 sittings, built in 1822 to designs by James Laurie, James McQueen and Authy McMillan (**fig 29**).[321] As is often the case, it was admired at the time, but less so later. In 1825 it was described as 'remarkably neat and spacious, and much superior to most of the parish kirks in this county',[322] but by 1906 it was said to be 'in striking contrast to the ornate ecclesiastical architecture of its neighbour, for it combines the appearance of a warehouse or factory with that of a barn'.[323] Its construction also involved the demolition of two standing arches seen by Pococke in 1760[324] and it overlay the site of the remains of the east range of the former cloister of the priory. 'We heard that disputes between the incumbent at the time and a factor with too much power had a good deal to do with the appearance of the building'. This refers to the square tower which had been added, leading to the comment that 'Of late years it has been improved a little'.[325] This church was altered in 1914 by P MacGregor Chalmers.[326] On completion of this new church, the old parish church in the nave of the medieval cathedral-priory was unroofed and left as a ruined shell in the kirkyard. The other major surviving component of the priory complex, the so-called commendator's house, was replaced by a new manse, described in 1839 as having been built 24 years ago, and being 'spacious and commodious'.[327] The old building became a school, eventually being demolished in the late nineteenth century. The cemetery extension to the east of the old kirkyard, and access from George Street (involving the demolition of a house), was paid for by the Marquess of Bute in the 1890s.[328]

As well as the parish church, there were by the 1830s two seceding congregations and a Roman Catholic one. The number of families attending them was: established church 420, Associate Synod 45, Cameronians 27 (these last two said in 1825 to have had no 'settled incumbent'), Roman Catholic 12, while the 'poor Irish' had no place of worship.[329] In social terms the Disruption did not have a major effect in Galloway. The number of Free Churches in the

FIGURE 29
The parish church, built
in 1822 on the site of the
east wing of the priory, its
pedestrian approach cutting
through the ruins of the
priory church (Paula Martin)

district is testimony to popular dissatisfaction with landowners' exercise of their rights to appoint ministers. Immediately after the Disruption a Free Church was built in King's Road in 1844.[330] Another was built at the same date at the Isle, on a site provided by Whithorn town council, in the harbour on land reclaimed below the high tide mark and so beyond the jurisdiction of the landowner (**fig 30**).[331] The range of churches increased in the later nineteenth century following a series of secessions from the already divided Church of Scotland. As well as the parish church and the Free Church, there was a new United Presbyterian church, built in 1892 in St John Street on the same site as its predecessor to a design by Thomson & Sandilands (it is now a garage) (**fig 31**),[332] and a Reformed Presbyterian (Cameronian) church (later the Drill Hall). By 1915, however, these two churches had merged to form the United Free Church.

The growing local Roman Catholic population also received formal provision in the form of an iron church out at High Mains, dedicated to Saints Ninian, Martin and John. Built in 1882, and paid for by the Marquess of Bute, this contained 120 sittings.[333] The church developed rapidly. Records of a St

Ninian's Day service there in 1892 point towards a place shaped for the Ninian cult in the confident revival of Roman Catholicism in late nineteenth-century Scotland.[334] Bute was also responsible for restoring a Premonstratensian presence to Galloway three centuries after the Reformation. He initially established a community at Craigeach Farm in Kirkcowan parish, which ran an agricultural training-school for orphan boys, and in 1889 he brought a short-lived community of canons to Whithorn.[335] It was perhaps typical of Bute's romantic medievalism that he wished to revive a monastic presence at one of the country's premier pre-Reformation shrines, but, despite the presence of a substantial local Roman Catholic population, practical ecclesiastical needs demanded development of a diocesan and parochial hierarchy rather than a monastic foundation; within a few years, the small community had withdrawn.

FIGURE 30
The former Free Church at Isle of Whithorn, built in 1844 on land built up from the harbour, and therefore the property of Whithorn burgh council, which owned the harbour but nothing else at the Isle (Paula Martin)

FIGURE 31
The former United Presbyterian Church, St John Street, built in 1892, and remarkably little altered by conversion to a feed store and later a garage (Colin Martin)

Other public buildings

Apart from the town house (see **fig 25**), early nineteenth-century Whithorn possessed no distinguished public buildings. As the nineteenth century progressed Whithorn gradually acquired more public buildings, but all were in keeping with the modest character of the town. Whithorn's precarious finances limited potential developments, and it was clearly difficult for it to keep up with changing requirements. This is demonstrated in the late provision of secure and suitable prison facilities. The prison within the town house was condemned in 1834. The Inspector's report of 1834, published in 1835, recorded that 'The town-house and gaol form a considerable building; notwithstanding which, *the gaoler does not reside within the gaol*, but at some distance, the spare rooms in the building being fitted up and let as *shops*'.[336] More modern prison accommodation, however, was not provided until the 1880s, when a police-house and prison was built to designs by David Henry of St Andrews at no. 29 St John Street.

For most of the nineteenth century the only large public meeting space was the council chamber on the first floor of the old town house. The new town hall, also in St John Street, and likewise designed by David Henry, was built by public subscription in 1885–86, at a cost of £1100, with a smaller hall added in 1898. It could hold about 500 people, and was described as 'plain but substantial'.[337] It was built purely to provide a public hall, and the council continued to meet and hold burgh courts in the old town house.[338] A subscription library survived into the twentieth century, though presumably replaced by the public library built in 1911, designed by Alexander Young, in St John Street (**fig 32**).[339] In 1839 there were two parochial schools (at Whithorn and the Isle) and nine others, plus four Sabbath schools.[340] Whithorn Academy was built on Castlehill in 1860–65, and was added to in 1895, 1899, 1907, and 1910.[341]

FIGURE 32
Public Library, St John Street,
built in 1911 (Paula Martin)

Domestic buildings

In the 1830s the main street was described as

> very irregular, being inconveniently narrow at both extremities, and
> uselessly wide in the middle … The dwelling-houses have been much
> improved since the termination of the war with France, many old ones
> having been pulled down, and new ones erected on the same site. This
> change seems rather to have been owing to the reduction of interest [on
> savings] than the demand for better dwellings, as many who had money
> in the banks were of opinion that it could be invested in houses to more
> advantage – which experience seems not to justify.[342]

By 1891 there were 298 houses, two being built, and another 27 vacant.
The *Ordnance Gazetteer* of 1895 reported 'great improvements' since the
beginning of the century, noting that 'The old thatched hovels have made

FIGURE 33
Nos 45–47 George Street,
built in 1901 as a grocery
shop, its size and imported
red sandstone surely a sign
of prosperity. It is now the
Whithorn Trust's Visitor
Centre (Paula Martin)

way for good slated houses, and the streets are no longer grass-grown'. In 1908 one writer commented on 'its ample thoroughfare and tidy appearance generally attracting the attention of visitors'[343] but to another commentator Whithorn consisted of 'featureless streets' within an 'uninteresting natural environment'. Although the economy of the town seems to have been in decline from the 1880s, one grocery was doing well enough to rebuild its premises at nos 45–47 George Street in 1901 (**fig 33**).[344]

Sport and recreation

Illustrating Victorian attitudes to self-help through personal connections, several masonic lodges, sporting and musical associations were formed. The Candida Casa lodge of Oddfellows was founded in 1873 with 30 members, and organised an annual parade and sports' day.[345] The Good Templar lodge was founded *c* 1900, and built the Belmont Hall, later used as the fire station.[346] In 1841 a total abstinence instrumental band was established, followed by a brass band in 1911. The bowling club opened in 1868, with a 'spacious and tastefully laid out bowling green' created in 1873 on ground provided at a nominal rent by the Earl of Galloway.[347] A curling club used an area to the north-west of the town known as Nummerston Loch, which has since been drained.[348] The golf club played on a nine-hole course laid out on a field behind Ketburn Place, and there was also a course just north of the Isle, which opened *c* 1900.[349] A football club had been established by the end of the nineteenth century.[350]

Population, immigration and occupations

Much of the development in public service provision appears to have been driven by a steady rise in population in both the burgh and the Isle over the nineteenth century. The generally upward trends noted in the 1790s and early 1800s continued, driven by an influx of immigrant labour from Ireland in the 1820s and again in the 1840s. The population profiles offered by trade directories suggest that there was a comparatively small professional and trade 'elite'. In 1825 there was only one resident gentry in Whithorn and five professionals (three surgeons, one physician, and one writer who was also the town clerk). Situated only ten miles from the county town, it would not have needed any more writers, but the number of doctors is high, and must reflect coverage of a wide area. There were 24 tradesmen, including 5 grocers, 4 drapers, 2 bakers, 2 boot- and shoe-makers, 2 watch-makers (1 also a plumber), a hat-maker, a spirit-dealer, and a tailor. There is a notable absence of building trades (but this would seem to be an accident of recording, given their prominence in trades lists of earlier and later dates). For the rest of the century trade directories show little change in economic activity or occupational balance within the town. Hints of broader horizons are gained from the wills of two men, in 1844 and 1863, both described as 'residing in

Jamaica, thereafter in Whithorn'.[351] In them, we can perhaps see traces of Whithorn's place within the expanding British Empire, with men who had made their money abroad returning to their place of origin later in life.

Whithorn's population expansion was matched by significant growth at the Isle. Indeed, in some ways the Isle was perhaps the more successful of the two locations. This is reflected in the profile of the population identifiable in the trade directories (**table 3**). In 1825 the Isle had two of the six resident gentry of the parish as a whole, and ten of the 34 shopkeepers/tradesmen (four grocers and six publicans).[352] In 1895 the Isle had 'some tasteful villas',[353] becoming, like Lochranza or Plockton, one of those places people chose to retire to, leading to an increase in house prices.[354]

The importance of the Isle to the parish is further demonstrated by data from wills. Of 173 surviving wills from between 1820 and 1901 of men living within the parish of Whithorn, with occupational descriptions, 70 were farmers, 36 in maritime occupations, 25 professionals, 22 merchants or shopkeepers, and 20 tradesmen.[355] These wills also provide evidence of links with other places through maritime commerce: two local men were masters of Liverpool ships; a Liverpool dockmaster and another former resident of Liverpool died at Whithorn; and the widow of a local master mariner died at Liverpool.[356] Other residents include a former warehouseman in Glasgow (1880), a second officer on a Port Glasgow ship (1886), a shipping agent from Ayr (1891), and a former resident of Greenock (1896).[357] In addition, there were links with Whitehaven.[358] The chronological spread of these records is shown in **table 4**.

TABLE 4
Chronological distribution of occupational data from testaments demonstrating the increase in maritime occupations in the second half of the nineteenth century, although testaments may have a time-lag between active occupation and death

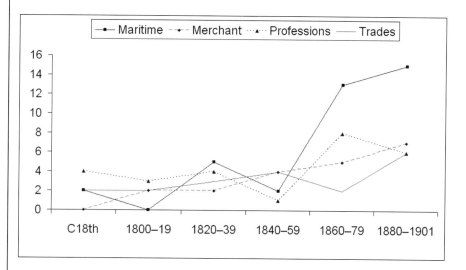

Gravestones, too, though not a statistically reliable source, serve to emphasise the important role maritime affairs played in the economy of the burgh. The number surviving in Whithorn, particularly for the nineteenth century, is relatively high. While they record a wide range of occupations, they are perhaps best seen not as a record of the numerical balance between occupations, but rather as highlighting those occupations which produced sufficient money to pay for the plot and the stone, and which therefore played a leading role in the economy of the town. What stands out from an analysis of the evidence is the importance of maritime-related occupations, and therefore the importance of the Isle, perhaps outweighing the balance of population between the two communities. The total number of recorded non-farming occupations is 132, the vast majority of these graves dating to the nineteenth century. They can be subdivided as: professionals 23 (17%), merchants/shopkeepers 18 (14%), tradesmen 24 (18%), miscellaneous 12 (9%), and 55 individuals with maritime-related occupations (42%). This final group comprises 49 mariners/master mariners/shipmasters, 3 customs/excise men, 1 coastguard, 1 harbourmaster, and 1 shipwright. Ages at death are recorded in 111 cases, the average age being 57, but for those who died at sea the average age was 27. The 38 who definitely or almost definitely lived at the Isle represent 29% of the total. Of these, all were seafarers except for a coastguard, a coastwaiter (customs official), a shipwright, two merchants and an innkeeper.[359] For the chronological spread of the data see **table 5**. The population of the Isle peaked in 1871 (**table 2**).

TABLE 5
Chronological distribution of occupational data from graveyard monuments demonstrating a peak in maritime occupations in the third quarter of the nineteenth century

A major change in the population profile of the parish began with the steady increase in Irish immigration into Scotland after *c* 1790, but particularly from *c* 1815 into the early 1850s. Originating as a seasonal movement of agricultural labourers, mainly harvest-workers, the migrants began to put down roots in south-western Scotland and established a distinct community. At first, these economic migrants did not move far beyond their point of arrival, creating social and economic strain in Galloway. Later many went further afield, seeking employment in factories in Glasgow, Paisley, and as far away as Dundee. The local minister in 1839 complained that there was too much emigration, and Irish immigration. 'These are,' he declared, 'possessed of nothing but a number of naked, starving children'.[360] His hostility towards the immigrants is particularly strident, even for an era noted for its bigotry and prejudice. A report in 1843 on poverty listed the numbers of Irish among the poor. In Whithorn 'many of the 5% poor in the town were Irish'.[361] Most were from Ulster, and the majority were Roman Catholics.

The religious needs of this floating Catholic population were served from 1819 by a priest based in Newton Stewart, who also held services in Whithorn, Stranraer and Kirkmaiden.[362] Some 25% of the immigrants were Protestants, however, and they brought with them several Ulster-Scots cultural institutions, including some of quite recent origin, such as the Loyal Orange Order.[363] The first Orange Lodge was established in Scotland in 1800 in Maybole, and by the 1830s there were Lodges in Wigtown, Kirkcudbright, Newton Stewart and Whithorn, as well as Glasgow and Paisley.[364]

To many Irish people the south-west was a staging-post. To contemporaries the problems they brought in their passage through the region were often more evident than the benefits.[365] While the large numbers may have been more perceived than real, it is certainly true that the Irish migrants were very poor. The south-west of Scotland was not a preferred destination, but it was the nearest and therefore the cheapest.[366] The introduction of steamships in the mid-nineteenth century meant that immigrants could travel direct to Glasgow, instead of landing in Ayrshire or Galloway, and this led to a falling away of immigration into the region.

The perception of Whithorn as a focus for Irish immigration was just one further image with which the community had to contend in the later nineteenth century. The crisis in the burgh's finances had meant that when most Scottish burghs were installing their post-cholera water supply and domestic sanitation systems, Whithorn remained dependent upon wells, street pumps and middens. As the population grew, these medieval arrangements must have become increasingly inadequate and overstrained. As a consequence, the burgh acquired an unsavoury reputation, as evident in one reference in 1908 to an apparently fairly recent past. 'Formerly its repute for repellent odours passed into local satiric rhyme, and association with the Irishry gave the little old town an undesirable notoriety. Under the beneficent influence of the modern Public Health Act, however, and stimulated by the general social advancement of Galloway, this pre-Reformation Mecca has outgrown its earliest unsavoury reputation'.[367] In 1901 Whithorn got its first gravitational water supply, improving the flow to the street pumps.[368] As the twentieth century dawned, Whithorn appeared finally to be acquiring the requisite trappings of a modern town.

1914 to the present

The impact of two World Wars, the shift from Empire to European Union, and the radical transformation of the basic structures of British society, can all be seen to have had significant effects on the life of Whithorn. The cost of war cannot be measured in the toll of lives alone, although the stark record of the war memorial, listing 69 men of the town who died in the First World War, and another twelve men from the Isle, gives some indication of the scale of the loss experienced, and the repercussions felt, in even this small, rural community. 'Built on the lines of the old Mercat Cross' in the middle of George Street, the memorial was unveiled by Sir Herbert Maxwell of Monreith in 1921.[369] A further nine men from Whithorn and five from the Isle, who died in the Second World War, are also commemorated. Although the loss of life was far greater in the First War, it was very much a remote conflict, the most obvious local manifestation of which may have been a shortage of manpower and an increase in the employment of women in agricultural work. In the Second World War, however, there was a direct military presence in the Machars, as a large military camp was opened in 1939 at Burrow Head, three miles south of Whithorn (see **map 2**).[370] Anti-aircraft gunners were trained there, involving the use of small boats based at the Isle and a slipway in front of the old lifeboat house. Even under wartime constraints, the presence of this base injected a significant volume of new money into the flagging local economy. It was boosted still further in the closing stages of the war when the coast from Garlieston southwards became a training area for the 1944 D-Day landings and a central location in the construction of the floating Mulberry Harbour which reinforced the invasion of Normandy.[371] Unfortunately for Whithorn, the end of warfare in 1945 saw a rapid running down of these facilities and the withdrawal of the added revenue which the military had brought.

Housing

The perennial problem of a lack of good-quality housing began to be addressed in 1935 with the erection of the first council houses in Wigtownshire villages, including Isle of Whithorn. Successive housing schemes have provided additional accommodation for the increased population, but in the 1950s there was still a housing shortage. Whithorn's housing stock was boosted by a row of prefabs at The Park, later replaced by more permanent bungalows on the same sites. Their earlier history is indicated by the reuse of several Anderson shelters as garden sheds (**fig 34**). In 1951 new housing was built to the south of the town, and by 1959 there were 328 inhabited houses, or 3.8% of the county total. Some 12% of the population of Whithorn lived more than two per room, the highest figure of the four burghs in the county. 'A number of [agricultural] workers reside in Whithorn or the Isle of Whithorn

FIGURE 34
One of several Anderson
shelters surviving in back
gardens in The Park
(Paula Martin)

and travel daily' on foot to farms without having to take tied housing.[372] In 1950, the *Official Guide* to the town reported proudly that 'A few years ago in a broadcast on "Slums of Scotland" the speaker held up the Royal Ancient burgh of Whithorn as a glowing example of what householders could do to beautify their town, for on a recent visit he had been struck by the cleanliness of its streets and the bright appearance of the houses which were all gaily painted, thus taking away any drabness and making the whole place most attractive'.[373]

Municipal services

The political upheavals of the middle decades of the twentieth century brought some of the most radical changes to affect Whithorn's status since the sixteenth century. In 1930 the town was officially reclassified as a 'small burgh', with fewer self-governing powers than the larger royal burghs and more powers taken over by the county council. While the change in status brought obvious benefits, the county council being able to provide services which the old burgh council could never have afforded, it was also the recognition of the end of the old regime. Whatever the impact of the change, especially with regard to the ancient rivalry with Wigtown, the new arrangements quickly began to produce benefits. Electricity and mains water came in 1935, sewerage in 1937 to Whithorn and 1940 to the Isle. Whithorn received part of its water supply from the county scheme and the Isle has a good gravitation system from Boyach Loch, improving the provision that had first been made at the beginning of the century.[374] The town had been lit by coal-gas from 1852, relatively late in Scotland, but before a rail connection was established to lower coal prices.[375] Continued development after the Second World War included the replacement by the Wigtownshire Electricity Company of gas street lights by electric lighting.[376]

The new county arrangements led gradually to changes in school provision. Centralisation and rationalisation began in Wigtownshire in the mid-1930s with the opening in 1935 of a central secondary school at Newton Stewart. As a result, Whithorn school first lost Latin from the curriculum, and although it was enlarged in 1958, became only a Junior Secondary before eventually losing its entire secondary department to Newton Stewart.[377] So the five schools in Whithorn and three in the Isle had been reduced by the 1960s to two, soon to be reduced to a single primary school in Whithorn itself.

Further local government changes after World War Two also had an impact on the burgh, most notably that Whithorn's boundary was extended in 1948.[378] In 1964 the counties of Galloway and Kirkcudbrightshire joined together for the provision of police and health services, and as a parliamentary constituency, while in 1975 major reorganisation of local government meant that administration was divided between Dumfries and Galloway Regional Council and Wigtown District Council, and the 'burgh' officially ceased to exist. In 1996 these authorities were replaced by a unitary Dumfries and Galloway Council.

The economy

The twentieth century can be seen very much as a period of continuing economic struggle for Whithorn. While the nature of the problems and the various responses to them may have changed substantially, the fact remains that Whithorn lost its *raison d'être* in the sixteenth century and, despite a whole succession of efforts to establish new, viable economic roles thereafter has struggled to survive. The critical factor has been the absence of any major exploitable resource in the burgh's hinterland which could have underpinned the development of an industrial base.

Agriculture remained, into the twentieth century, the primary employer and dominant sector of the local economy, exposing Whithorn and the southern Machars to every shift in agricultural fortunes. There were attempts at diversification, or more particularly at innovation, within the established farming practices. Traditionally this was, by the later nineteenth century, an area of mixed farming with a bias towards livestock. This bias increased at the end of the nineteenth century with the introduction of dairying and for the burgh was reflected in the opening in 1902 of the Whithorn creamery. As with earlier developments, the initiative was well-intentioned and optimistic, but 'In spite of improved marketing of produce, the establishment of creameries, and selective breeding, the economic position of the dairy industry [in Galloway] was relatively unstable during the period 1880–1930'.[379] The creamery, positioned at the end of an extended rail link, struggled to be a viable commercial operation until a degree of central planning and broader strategy led to the establishment in 1933 of the Scottish Milk Marketing Board. Subsequently taken over by the Scottish Co-operative Wholesale Society, the creamery survived until 1973, when work was transferred to the Milk Marketing Board's plant in Sorbie, also now defunct.[380] Part of the Glebe Field site in Whithorn was developed as a market garden in the later nineteenth century and continued to function as such into the early 1980s.[381]

In an age where road transport was increasingly dominant, Whithorn's perceived isolation became a growing deterrent to inward investment. While more money was spent on upgrading the road network after the county council took over responsibility for the roads in the 1930s, even better quality roads could not stimulate much improvement in the local economic position, especially when paralleled by a continued decline in the fortunes of the railway. Although large numbers of passengers could, on occasions such as the Roman Catholic pilgrimages to Whithorn in the 1930s, still arrive by train, such infrequent demand could not save the branch line during the programme of rationalisation which followed the nationalisation of the railways after the Second World War. The cuts were progressive, the last passenger train running in 1950 and the last goods train in 1964.[382] The station buildings were removed c 1972.[383] Shorn of both rail and maritime links, and lying at the end of a long and slow road from the regional trunk-road network, Whithorn and the southern Machars generally have struggled to attract investment.

The only significant 'industrial' concern in Whithorn was a small and relatively short-lived carpet factory in the old Free Church in King's Road. Despite the parish's extensive coastline and the presence of a good harbour at the Isle, no marine industries made a significant economic presence in the twentieth century. The area had never developed a serious fishing industry, although there was and is salmon netting on the Cree.[384] The lifeboat station at the Isle closed in 1919, being replaced by a motor vessel based at Kirkcudbright.[385] The coastguard station, from 1923 under the auspices of the Board of Trade, continued as one of five bases within the Solway sector of the organisation. The harbour, like many others of a similar size around the Scottish coast, ceased to handle trading vessels, but retained a few boats involved in small-scale trawling and lobster fishing, and has now become home to many pleasure craft. In 1969 part of the pier collapsed during a storm, and, since the harbour was not considered to be a strategic economic asset, much community effort was needed to persuade the county council to repair it. Like all seagoing communities, the Isle has seen its share of accidents and deaths at sea: in 2000 the village suffered a major loss with the sinking of the *Solway Harvester* off the Isle of Man. The crew of seven, three from the Isle, three from Whithorn and one from Garlieston, all died.

Service, not industry or commerce, remained the principal function of the burgh in the twentieth century. In the 1950s trade was said to be good, the various shops being 'well supported by both burgh and country residents',[386] while a local guidebook from the 1950s observed that 'Whithorn is an excellent shopping centre. Although some of its shops retain their old world exteriors the interiors are surprisingly modern and extensive and wide ranges of goods of every description are carried. Agencies for every well-known firm are held by various shopkeepers'.[387] It is in this local retail sector that Whithorn continues to serve the south Machars.

Tourism and pilgrimages

Industry and agriculture failing to contribute much to the burgh's economy, others looked to tourism to provide a boost. Visitor numbers, however, were low, and there was little investment in new accommodation or other tourist provisions. If anything, there was a reduction in hotel accommodation in

Whithorn itself, with only two hotels recorded in the 1950s, the Station Road and the Grapes, both of which had been originally intended to serve commercial travellers. The Second World War also saw the demise of both the tennis courts and the nine-hole golf course. King's Road now housed a 'very modern' Picture House.[388] Clearly, there were efforts to improve the facilities on offer to local residents, largely reflecting the social policies of the 1930s and changing tastes in entertainment. In St John Street, for example, attached to the County Library was 'a fine Billiard Room', while the 'new town hall' had an 'excellent modern dance floor'.[389]

What emerged gradually, however, was a realisation of the significance of the place itself, and the economic potential of this significance. In 1954, for example, one guidebook commented that Whithorn had a similar significance for Christianity in Scotland to that of Philippi in Greece or Kiev in Russia,[390] an observation that while not untrue gives a somewhat exaggerated sense of the burgh's status in later twentieth-century Scotland. Nevertheless, the town was regaining a sense of its historic importance, though this led to a mistaken boast that it was 'one of oldest royal burghs in Scotland'.[391] The excavations at the priory and the chapel at the Isle directed by Ralegh Radford on behalf of the Ministry of Works from 1948 to 1953, followed by Roy Ritchie's work between 1957 and 1967, served to reinforce this heightened sense of historic significance. The conversion in 1908 of the Old School, with its datestone of 1731, into a museum for displaying the excavated remains represented the beginnings of an effort to turn the archaeological and historical heritage of Whithorn into a tourist attraction. This was a powerful incentive in the development of the Whithorn Excavation Committee in the late 1980s and early 1990s.[392]

The Isle was also seeking to establish a tourist-based economy. In 1915 the Isle had two hotels, provided originally for commercial travellers, but only one boarding house and one set of apartments to let. Nevertheless, it has been described as 'a great resort of holiday-makers in pre-war days'.[393] In the 1940s the 'castle' was still a boarding house,[394] but the main development of tourism in the Isle post-dates the Second World War and is principally post-1970. The optimistic construction of a holiday village on the northern side of the Isle in the 1970s was a manifestation of confidence in its potential as a yachting marina, but its continued perceived remoteness by road has seen it lose out to better-served competitors, notably Kirkcudbright and Kippford in the Solway and Troon in the Clyde estuary.

One of the most significant 'tourist' developments at Whithorn in the first half of the twentieth century was the revival of the annual Roman Catholic pilgrimage to the site of St Ninian's shrine. There had, apparently, been small-scale visits to Whithorn by local schoolchildren from about 1912, but a large, formal event was first planned in 1924.[395] Organised from the diocesan centre in Dumfries, it saw 700 pilgrims arrive by train in the town, while perhaps another 2000 came by road. It was possibly the most significant gathering to have occurred in Whithorn for over 350 years, attended by the Marquess of Bute and the Duke and Duchess of Norfolk, the premier lay Roman Catholics in Scotland and England. Pilgrims walked from the priory via High Mains to St Ninian's Cave. By the 1930s, the pilgrimage had established itself as an annual event which drew crowds of over 3000, who arrived in Whithorn by road and rail. These pilgrims, although mainly day-trippers, provided a significant boost to the local economy. In 1932 representatives of the Church of Scotland and the Episcopal Church gathered to mark the 1500th anniversary of the death of St Ninian. The outbreak of war in 1939, however, brought an end to such gatherings. The pilgrimage resumed after 1945 and drew large crowds during the 1950s, with some 6000 attending in 1959. A high

FIGURE 35
The Hew Lorimer sculpture above the open-air altar at the back of the Roman Catholic church
(Paula Martin)

point was the 1997 pilgrimage to celebrate the notional 1600th anniversary of Ninian's arrival in Galloway.[396]

The Roman Catholic congregation, despite the revival of pilgrimage, worshipped in the corrugated-iron church of Saints Ninian, Martin and John until it was eventually replaced by a building designed by Goodhart-Rendel, Broadbent & Curtis in 1959–60.[397] This new building stands near the site of the pre-1814 tolbooth in a newly created gap in the south-east wall of George Street. It was a formal sign of the integration of the Roman Catholic congregation within the wider community. Rather formal and old-fashioned, as one might expect of this Arts and Crafts architect from London, the church has an open-air altar to the rear, backed by a sculpture by Hew Lorimer (**fig 35**). Close to this altar are some fragments of carved stonework from the medieval cathedral.

The revival of Roman Catholic pilgrimage to Whithorn reflects just one aspect of the continuing religious change in Scotland generally during the twentieth century. The religious profile of the burgh was reshaped in a number of stages as the denominational structure altered. A succession of reunions and fresh schisms in the various Presbyterian churches in the aftermath of the 1843 Disruption began to resolve itself in the first half of the twentieth century, with implications for the provision of church buildings in Whithorn. After the United Presbyterians had joined the Free Church in 1900 and the Free Church rejoined the Church of Scotland in 1929, the St John Street church became redundant and was sold off to become first a feed store, and later a garage (**fig 31**).[398] The former Reformed Presbyterian Church became the Drill Hall for the Territorial Army, while the former Free Church in King Street served as the hall for the parish church. The former Free Church at Isle of Whithorn now serves the southern half of the parish (which is combined with Glasserton).

Conclusion

In the early twenty-first century, Whithorn is a local service centre for a compact hinterland. There is hope for further potential tourist development, founded on the identification of Whithorn as the 'cradle of Scottish Christianity', but the tourist 'draw' is still perhaps hindered by the perception of the physical remoteness of the burgh from major communication links and from other significant tourist centres, yet without the romance of the even more remote Iona.

Attempts at small-scale industrial development have come and gone with successive government schemes designed to encourage investment, a problem not confined to Whithorn but common to much of the rest of Galloway. Unemployment remains a problem, particularly because of the continuing reliance in the region on agriculture and forestry, no longer labour-intensive occupations. The continuing fragility of the agricultural economy in the post-Chernobyl, post-BSE, post-foot-and-mouth environment serves also to underline the almost total dependence of Whithorn on its rural hinterland. Employment opportunities, or the lack of them, have seen a progressive drifting away of the younger population. This significant restructuring of the demographic profile has been accentuated by the inward migration of a large retirement and second-home-owning segment.

Notes

1   S Ramsay, J Miller, J, and R Housely, nd, Whithorn Environs: Palaeoenvironmental Investigation of Rispain Mire (first draft, Dept of Archaeology, University of Glasgow)

2   NMRS records NX44SW 16–18, NX44SE 5

3   NMRS record NX44SW 19

4   NMRS records NX44SW 36, NX44SE 14 (fragment, now missing) and 15 (now in Museum)

5   J Morrison, 2001, An Archaeological Evaluation at Whithorn, Dumfries & Galloway. Unpublished report, Headland Archaeology Ltd; J Morrison, 2003, Research and Training Excavation in the Manse Field, Whithorn, Dumfries & Galloway: Data Structure Report. Unpublished report, Headland Archaeology Ltd

6   NMRS record NX44SW 45 and 46; it is suggested that these two records may refer to a single axe, but the sizes are different

7   NMRS record NX43NE 11

8   NMRS record NX43NE 8

9   R Toolis, 2003, 'A survey of the promontory forts of the North Solway coast', *TDGNHAS* 77, 50–1

10   NMRS record NX43NE 14

11   NMRS record NX43NE 39

12   eg C Thomas, 1992, *Whithorn's Christian Beginnings. First Whithorn Lecture 19th September 1992* (Friends of the Whithorn Trust, 1992), 16

13   NMRS records NX44SE 6, NX44SW 8, 15, 19

14   Thomas, *Whithorn's Christian Beginnings*, 19. The Roman cremation burials are not so far attested in the 2006 assessment of excavation records. Also relating to the Roman period is an Iron Age defended farm 1 mile west of Whithorn at Rispain, excavated in 1978–79, possibly the home farm of a minor Iron Age chief of the early centuries AD. The Novantae tribe is mentioned by Roman sources

15   P Hill, *Whithorn and St Ninian. The Excavation of a Monastic Town, 1984–91* (The Whithorn Trust & Sutton Publishing, Stroud, 1997), 292–7

16   Hill, *Whithorn*, 26; see below

17   Hill, *Whithorn*, 8–11. A more detailed report has now been published on the Ritchie excavations of 1957–67: C Lowe (ed), *Clothing for the Soul Divine – Burials at the tomb of St Ninian. Excavations at Whithorn Priory, 1957–1967* (Historic Scotland Archaeology Report **3**, 2009)

18   Hill, *Whithorn*

19   Pollock, *Whithorn 5*; Pollock, *Whithorn 6*; Clarke, *Whithorn 7*

20   C Lowe, Early Ecclesiastical Enclosures at Whithorn: an archaeological
       assessment (Unpublished report, Headland Archaeology Ltd, 2001); Morrison,
       Archaeological Evaluation; Morrison, Manse Field

21   Hill, *Whithorn*, 10

22   Pollock, *Whithorn 5*; Pollock, *Whithorn 6*; Clarke, *Whithorn 7*

23   A Nicholson, Whithorn Watching Brief: November 1998/January 1999
       (Unpublished report by Wigtownshire Archaeology Associates for British
       Telecom, 1999), Intervention B

24   P Harrington, Scottish Power's Electricity Pole and Stave Block Trenches,
       Whithorn (Unpublished report for Dumfries and Galloway SMR, 1992)

25   Hill, *Whithorn*

26   Lowe, Early Ecclesiastical Enclosures

27   Morrison, Archaeological Evaluation

28   Morrison, Manse Field

29   http://www.whithornpriorymuseum.gov.uk/whithorn/whithornhome.htm

30   Hill, *Whithorn*, 5, 53

31   Hill, *Whithorn*, 6 and fig 1.4

32   NMRS record NX43NW 9

33   Further stones from the interior have been removed to Whithorn Museum
       and the National Museum of Scotland. Much of the 'cave' has now been
       destroyed by a rockfall, leaving a small depression.

34   Nicholson, Watching Brief, Intervention C

35   *Discovery and Excavation in Scotland*, 2003, 7; *DES*, 2004, 40

36   *DES*, 2002, 31

37   Pollock, *Whithorn 5*

38   Pollock, *Whithorn 6*

39   Clarke, *Whithorn 7*

40   Morrison, Manse Field

41   *DES*, 1998, 30

42   M'Kerlie, *Lands and their Owners*, 471. The team inspected the site in March
       2006, and were convinced it was not a castle site

43   M'Kerlie, *Lands and Their Owners*, 418–19

44   A P Smyth, *Warlords and Holy Men: Scotland AD 80–1000* (London, 1984), 22–4;
       D Brooke, 'The Northumbrian Settlements in Galloway and Carrick: an
       Historical Assessment', *PSAS* 121 (1991), 300–1

45   Brooke, 'Northumbrian Settlements', 301–24

46   Smyth, *Warlords and Holy Men*, 27–9

47   See, Hill, *Whithorn*, 16–22; J MacQueen, 'The Literary Sources for the Life of
       St Ninian', in R Oram and G Stell (eds), *Galloway: Land and Lordship*, 17–25; D
       Craig, 'Pre-Norman Sculpture in Galloway: Some Territorial Implications', in
       R Oram and G Stell (eds), Galloway: *Land and Lordship*, 49–53

48   R D Oram, 'Scandinavian settlement in south-west Scotland with a special
       study of Bysbie', in B E Crawford (ed), *Scandinavian Settlement in Northern
       Britain* (London, 1995), 127–40. For the context of the Scandinavian

settlement, see R D Oram, *The Lordship of Galloway* (Edinburgh, 2000), 1–50, 247–50

49   R D Oram, 'Heirs to Ninian: the medieval bishops of Whithorn (*c*.1128 to 1560)', in R McCluskey (ed), *The See of Ninian: A History of the Medieval Diocese of Whithorn and the Diocese of Galloway in Modern Times* (Ayr, 1997), 51–2

50   *Njal's Saga*, trans M Magnusson and H Pálsson (Harmondsworth, 1960), 353

51   See the discussion in Oram, *Lordship of Galloway*, 13–15

52   See Oram, *Lordship of Galloway*, 10–11

53   *Historians of the Church of York and Its Archbishops*, ii, ed J Raine (London, 1894), 48–9

54   *Historians of York*, ii, 60

55   For the development of the lordship of Galloway and the career of Fergus see, Oram, *Lordship of Galloway*, chapters 1, 2 and 6

56   Oram, *Lordship of Galloway*, 171

57   Oram, *Lordship of Galloway*, 15–18

58   Oram, *Lordship of Galloway*, 223–4; G Ewart, *Cruggleton Castle* (Dumfries, 1986)

59   C A Ralegh Radford and G Donaldson, *Whithorn and Kirkmadrine* (HMSO, 1953), 28–30; C A Ralegh Radford, 'Cruggleton Church', *TDGNHAS*, 3rd ser, xxviii (1949–50), 92–5; C A Ralegh Radford, 'The Churches of Dumfriesshire and Galloway', *TDGNHAS*, 3rd ser, xl (1961–62), 102–16; D MacGibbon and T Ross, *The Ecclesiastical Architecture of Scotland*, i (Edinburgh, 1896), 212–15

60   Ralegh Radford and Donaldson, *Whithorn and Kirkmadrine*, 15–16

61   Oram, *Lordship of Galloway*, 182–7

62   For a detailed discussion of the consequences of Alan's death, see Oram, *Lordship of Galloway*, chapter 5

63   Analysis of Alexander II's policies is given in R D Oram, 'Introduction: an Overview of the Reign of Alexander II', in R D Oram (ed), *The Reign of Alexander II* (Leiden, 2005), 22–8 and 41–2

64   Oram, *Lordship of Galloway*, 182–6. The disputed election of 1235 is discussed in detail in A Ashley, 'Odo, Elect of Whithern, 1235', *TDGNHAS*, 3rd ser, xxxvii (1958–59), 62–9; R J Brentano, 'Whithorn and York', *SHR* (1953), 144–6, and 'The Whithorn Vacancy', *Innes Review*, iv (1953), 71–83. References in the documents relating to the canons' election of Odo Ydonc against Alexander's nominee, Gilbert, monk of Melrose, to 'the war of the king of Scots against Galloway', and 'the king of Scots, who now holds Galloway', allude to the invasion of the lordship and the ruthless suppression of the rising there (see *Register of Walter Gray, Lord Archbishop of York*, ed J Raine (Surtees Society, 1870), ii, 170–3)

65   R D Oram, 'Bruce, Balliol and the lordship of Galloway', *TDGNHAS*, 3rd ser, lxvii (1992), 29–47; R D Oram, 'Dervorgilla, the Balliols and Buittle', *TDGNHAS*, 3rd ser, lxxiii (1999), 165–81

66   *The Exchequer Rolls of Scotland*, ed J Stuart *et al* (Edinburgh, 1878–1908), i, 39; Oram, 'Bruce, Balliol and Galloway', 30–1

67 *Register of John le Romeyn, Lord Archbishop of York*, i (Surtees Society, 1913), 8–9, 83–5

68 R D Oram, *A Monastery and its Landscape: Whithorn and Monastic Estate Management in Galloway c 1250–c 1600* (Friends of the Whithorn Trust, 2005), currently provides the most detailed exploration of the priory estate in the later medieval period

69 Ralegh Radford and Donaldson, *Whithorn and Kirkmadrine*, 23

70 K Veitch, 'The conversion of native religious communities to the Augustinian Rule in twelfth- and thirteenth-century Alba', *Records of the Scottish Church History Society*, xxix (1999), 1–22; Ralegh Radford and Donaldson, *Whithorn and Kirkmadrine*, 15–16; D E Easson, *Medieval Religious Houses: Scotland* (London, 1957), 88

71 R Fawcett and R D Oram, *Dryburgh Abbey* (Stroud, 2005), 129–30 and see also figs 1 (Abbey of Prémontré) and 10 (plan of Alnwick Abbey). No excavation work has been undertaken to determine whether or not a west range existed at any period at Whithorn, but the dimensions of the east range and the nave of the church, if projected into a square cloister garth, do not allow room for a structural western quarter, but would allow simply a screen wall, as appears to have been the case at Alnwick, Dryburgh and Prémontré itself. Most modern interpretational plans of the priory ruins are careful to avoid showing any range in this quarter, eg the plan offered in the revised C A Ralegh Radford and G Donaldson, *Whithorn and the Ecclesiastical Monuments of Wigtown District* (Edinburgh, 1984), 16, but the plans given in Hill, *Whithorn*, eg figs 2.23 and 2.24 give a rectangular shape to the cloister garth and leave open the possibility that there may have been a fully developed western range at some stage, as shown in the conjectural reconstruction in fig 2.25

72 C A Ralegh Radford, 'Excavations at Whithorn (Final Report)', *TDGNHAS*, 3rd ser, xxxiv (1955–6), 131–94

73 Hill, *Whithorn*, 60–5

74 *Reg. Gray*, 172

75 *Reg. Romeyn*, 8–9, 83–5

76 *RMS*, i, *1306–1424*, ed J M Thomson (repr. Edinburgh, 1984), appendix I, no. 21

77 *The Legends of SS Ninian and Machor*, ed W M Metcalfe (Edinburgh, 1904), 68

78 *Wigtownshire Charters*, ed R C Reid (Scottish History Society, 1960), no. 1

79 *RMS*, ii, *1424–1513*, ed J Balfour Paul (repr. Edinburgh, 1984), no. 12

80 *Calendar of Scottish Supplications to Rome 1428–1432*, eds A I Dunlop and I B Cowan (SHS, 1970), 175–6. The supplication gives interesting details of the nature of the services performed in the chapel, which appears to have been intended principally as a chantry chapel for Prior Thomas

81 *Wigtownshire Chrs*, no. 6

82 Ralegh Radford and Donaldson, *Whithorn and Kirkmadrine*, 31–2

83 *Calendar of Entries in the Papal Registers Relating to Britain and Ireland: Papal Letters*, xii, *1458–1471*, ed J A Twemlow (London, 1933)

84 *TA*, i, *1473–1498*, ed T Dickson (Edinburgh, 1877), 182

85 *TA*, ii, 104, 157

86   *TA*, ii, 72

87   *TA*, iii, 280

88   Yeoman, *Pilgrimage*, 39–41

89   R D Oram, P F Martin, C A McKean, A Cathcart and T Neighbour, *Historic Tain* (2009). Separate payments at this chapel were also made in July 1505 (*TA*, iii, 62), August 1506 (*TA*, iii, 280), July 1507 (*TA*, iii, 291). It has been suggested that this 'chapel on the hill' referred to a site at Mains Farm, south-west of the burgh, where the 'Peter' stone had originally stood. The farm was bought in the late nineteenth century by the Marquis of Bute for a new Roman Catholic place of worship in a revival of the believed early medieval location of a chapel here. There is, however, no mention of such a chapel in any surviving pre-Reformation documents

90   *TA*, ii, 104; *TA*, iii, 375

91   See, for example, R Fawcett and R Oram, *Melrose Abbey* (Stroud, 2004), 57, 197

92   *Wigtownshire Chrs*, no. 27

93   M Dilworth, *Scottish Monasteries in the Late Middle Ages* (Edinburgh, 1995), 50

94   *The Heads of Religious Houses in Scotland from the Twelfth to Sixteenth Centuries*, eds D E R Watt and N F Shead (Scottish Record Society, 2001), 219

95   Dilworth, *Scottish Monasteries*, 80

96   D Brooke, *The Medieval Cult of St Ninian* (Friends of the Whithorn Trust, 1988), 4

97   Dilworth, *Scottish Monasteries*, 82 and map 5; Ralegh Radford and Donaldson, *Whithorn and Kirkmadrine*, 25

98   *RRS*, v, *The Acts of Robert I*, ed A A M Duncan (Edinburgh, 1988), no. 275

99   *RRS*, v, 110 and nos 19 and 20 (April 1312), Edward witnessed two charters as 'lord of Galloway'

100   M Maclennan, *A Pronouncing and Etymological Dictionary of the Gaelic Language* (repr. Aberdeen, 1988), 85

101   Hill, *Whithorn*, chapter 6

102   The dates of the week-long fair were confirmed in 1459 as 25 August, the Vigil of the Blessed Ninian, and the three days either side (*RMS*, ii, no. 733). In 1511, however, the date changed so that the fair began on 29 June, St Peter's Day (*RMS*, ii, 3569)

103   *Wigtownshire Chrs*, no. 1

104   *Wigtownshire Chrs*, no. 2

105   *Wigtownshire Chrs*, no. 8. The sources do not make clear how correct his statement was

106   *Wigtownshire Chrs*, no. 9

107   *Wigtownshire Chrs*, no. 11

108   *Wigtownshire Chrs*, no. 12

109   *Wigtownshire Chrs*, no. 13

110   *Wigtownshire Chrs*, no. 32. For Duncan McGown's activities as a merchant, see below

111   *RMS*, ii, no. 383

112   *RMS*, ii, no. 453

113   *Wigtownshire Chrs*, no. 109

114 *RMS*, ii, no. 3569

115 *Wigtownshire Chrs*, no. 111

116 *Wigtownshire Chrs*, no. 110

117 *Wigtownshire Chrs*, no. 113. This was a reissue of royal burgh status following the destruction of the Black Douglases and annexation of their estates to the crown in 1455. Wigtown had been granted to Malcolm Fleming as a component of his earldom of Wigtown by David II in 1341 (*RRS*, vi, no. 39) and placed under his regality jurisdiction. The implication of this is that it had lost its 'royal' status, no longer being an immediate crown tenant, and that it had passed as a burgh in barony or regality from the Flemings to the Black Douglases with the earldom in the 1370s, a status confirmed by royal charter to William, 8th Earl of Douglas, in October 1451 (*RMS*, ii, no. 503). Earlier charters bestowing royal burgh status had presumably been cancelled and the new grant gave Wigtown an ancestry extending back only a little more than half a century at the date of their complaint

118 *Wigtownshire Chrs*, no. 114a

119 *TA*, v, 455

120 *Wigtownshire Chrs*, no. 115

121 *Wigtownshire Chrs*, no. 116a

122 *RPC*, vi, *1599–1604*, ed D Masson (Edinburgh, 1884), vi, 27

123 *Calendar of Documents Relating to Scotland*, ii, 1272–1307, ed J Bain (Edinburgh, 1884), no. 1225

124 *RRS*, vi, nos 367–73

125 *RMS*, ii, no. 107

126 *TA*, ii, 458

127 'Ninian', in *Legends of the Saints in the Scots Dialect of the Fourteenth Century*, ed W M Metcalfe, iii (Edinburgh, 1891), 304–45

128 *Legends of the Saints*, 325–7

129 *Legends of the Saints*, 343–7

130 *Calendar of Scottish Supplications to Rome*, iv, *1433–1447*, eds A I Dunlop and D MacLauchlan (Glasgow, 1983), no. 746

131 D Mackay, 'The Four Heid Pilgrimages of Scotland', *Innes Review*, xix (1968)

132 *TA*, ii, 443

133 For expenses incurred in preparation of her household for the journey, see *TA*, i, 29, 44

134 *TA*, i, 91

135 *TA*, i, 172. For James IV at Tain, see Oram *et al*, *Tain*; J Durkan, 'The sanctuary and college of Tain', *Innes Review*, xiii (1962), 147–56

136 *TA*, i, 385; *TA*, ii, 104. He paid 28s to two other lutars 'that passit to Quhithirn' on 9 May 1501 (*TA*, ii, 107)

137 *TA*, ii, 113, 159

138 *TA*, iii, 375. The minstrels accompanied the royal couple throughout the entire pilgrimage in July 1507 (*TA*, iii, 399)

139 *TA*, ii, 41

140 *TA*, i, 182

141 *TA*, i, 358, 385; *TA*, iii, 155

142 *TA*, i, 355–6, 385

143 *TA*, ii, 251

144 *TA*, ii, 72, 81

145 Eg *TA*, ii, 249, 251; *TA*, iv, 107

146 *TA*, ii, 442

147 *TA*, ii, 442; *TA*, iii, 152; Hill, *Whithorn*, 394

148 *TA*, iii, 73; *TA*, iv, 39

149 Oram *et al*, *Tain*

150 *TA*, v, 276–7

151 A Fraser, *Mary Queen of Scots* (London, 1969), 216

152 Oram, 'Heirs to Ninian', 79–80

153 Ralegh Radford and Donaldson, *Whithorn and Kirkmadrine*, 26

154 Ralegh Radford and Donaldson, *Whithorn and Kirkmadrine*, 26

155 Ralegh Radford and Donaldson, *Whithorn and Kirkmadrine*, 26

156 *RPC*, vi, 405

157 *RPC*, vi, 808

158 *RPC*, xi, 154

159 *Fasti Ecclesiae Scoticanae Medii Aevi ad Annum 1638*, ed D E R Watt (Scottish Record Society, 1969), 13; Ralegh Radford and Donaldson, *Whithorn and Kirkmadrine*, 26

160 Watt, *Fasti*, 133

161 J Gifford, *The Buildings of Scotland: Dumfries and Galloway* (London, 1996), 564

162 Ralegh Radford, C A, 'Excavations at Whithorn', 131–94

163 *RRS*, v, no. 275

164 *TA*, ii, 72; *TA*, iii, 62; *TA*, iii, 280; *TA*, iii, 291

165 *A Diurnal of Remarkable Occurrents That Have Passed Within the Country of Scotland Since the Death of King James IV till the Year 1575* (Bannatyne Club, 1833), 21

166 *Wigtownshire Chrs*, 14

167 *RPS*, vii, *1575–1580*, ed G Donaldson (Edinburgh, 1966), no. 2024, see also no. 2119

168 NAS GD30/1967 dated 14/6/1587. An account and reckoning of the mails due from the Isle had been drawn up between Sharp and the Martins on 17 January 1587 (GD30/610)

169 NAS GD30/936 dated 3/8/1584

170 NAS GD30/393 dated 30/10/1595

171 *CSP*, iii, 1569–1571, ed W K Boyd (Edinburgh, 1903), 255

172 *CSP*, iv, 77

173 *CSP*, x, 241–2, 257, 259, 837–8, 851–3, 856

174 *Calendar of Documents Relating to Scotland*, v, 1108–1516 (Supplementary), eds G G Simpson and J D Galbraith (Edinburgh, 1985), no. 1080

175 *RMS*, ii, no. 2075, Patrick Makilwion, John Marsell, Gilbert Frussel and Thomas Makonyll

176 *RMS*, ii, no. 2486

177 *Wigtownshire Chrs*, no. 109

178 *RMS*, ii, no. 3569

179   *Wigtownshire Chrs*, no. 110

180   *Wigtownshire Chrs*, no. 112

181   *TA*, i, 240

182   *RPS*, viii, no. 2462

183   *Wigtownshire Chrs*, no. 17

184   *RPC*, ii, 636, 644–7

185   Chadburn, 'Building Stone Sources'

186   *CSP*, iii, 255

187   *RPC*, xi, 154

188   *RPC*, vi, 384

189   *RPC*, vi, 818

190   *RPC*, 2nd ser, i, 463–4

191   *RPC*, 2nd ser, i, 621

192   *RPC*, 3rd ser, iii, 501–2

193   *RPC*, 2nd ser, i, 626

194   J A Russell, *The Book of Galloway* (Dumfries, 1962), 54

195   For a very partial account of the rising, see Sir James Turner, *Memoirs of His Own Life and Times, MDCXXXII–MDCLXX* (Bannatyne Club, 1829)

196   M'Kerlie, *Lands and their Owners*, 421

197   Andrew Symson, *A Large Description of Galoway by Andrew Symson, Minister of Kirkinner, 1684* (Edinburgh, 1823), 46

198   *RPC*, 3rd ser, viii, 329. The contributions from selected royal burghs in 1684 were, in descending order of magnitude: Edinburgh £33 6s 8d, Glasgow £15, Aberdeen £6, Dundee £5, Ayr £1 14s 8d, Dumfries £1 13s 4d, Irvine 18s, Kirkcudbright 16s, Wigtown 8s, Annan 2s, Kilrenny 2s, Kintore 2s, Stranraer 2s, **Whithorn 2s**

199   'Register Containing the State and Condition of every Burgh within the Kingdom of Scotland … 1692', in *Miscellany of the Scottish Burgh Records Society* (Edinburgh, 1881), 134–6. For comparison, the income of Kirkcudbright was about £880 Scots, Wigtown £693 13s 4d, and Stranraer £143 16s 8d

200   Symson, *Galoway*

201   Ralegh Radford, 'Whithorn (Final Report)'

202   Symson, *Galoway*, 46

203   *CRB*, iii, 413, 515

204   *CRB*, iv, 5, 10, 21

205   RCAHMS, *Tolbooths and Townhouses: Civic Architecture in Scotland to 1883* (HMSO, 1996), 200

206   H C Jones, *The Wigtownshire Hearth Tax Collection Lists of 1692* (Greenbrook, Australia, 1979)

207   T C Smout, *Scottish Trade on the Eve of Union, 1660–1707* (Edinburgh, 1963); L M Cullen, 'Incomes, social classes and economic growth in Ireland and Scotland, 1600–1900' in T M Devine and D Dickson (eds), *Ireland and Scotland 1600–1850* (Edinburgh, 1983), 248–60; C A Whatley, 'Taking Stock: Scotland at the End of the Seventeenth Century', in T C Smout (ed), *Anglo-Scottish Relations from 1603 to 1900* (Oxford, 2005)

208 Symson, *Galoway*, 46

209 Rupert Houseley's palaeoenvironmental analysis of Rispain Moss points to
the systematic stripping of viably extractable peat supplies from the whole of
the upper reaches of the Ket valley, presumably through demand from both
Whithorn and neighbouring proprietors and farm tenants; see Ramsay *et al*,
'Palaeoenvironmental Investigations of Rispain Mire'

210 The Murrays of Broughton and Cally, for example, were enclosing their lands
in Whithorn parish in the 1730s and renting them out as cattle parks (NAS
GD10/1299)

211 I Donnachie and I MacLeod, *Old Galloway* (Newton Abbot, 1974), 12

212 J Webster, *General View of the Agriculture of Galloway* (Edinburgh, 1794), 2, 4–5

213 Webster, *Agriculture of Galloway*, 21, 29

214 *History of the Union of Scotland and England by Sir John Clerk of Pennicuik*,
trans and ed D Duncan (SHS, 1993), 2–4. For Clerk's involvement in Scottish
national financial matters, see GD18/3128, Copy Minute Book of the
Commissioners of Parliament for examination of public accounts, 1703–04

215 P Martin, Cupar, Fife, 1700–*c* 1820, a small Scottish town in an era of change
(unpublished PhD thesis, University of Dundee, 2000), 328 n.101, Cupar,
for example, had a gap between September 1715 and October 1716 in town
council minutes, and October 1715 and February 1716 in presbytery minutes

216 B Lenman, *The Jacobite Risings in Britain 1689–1746* (Aberdeen, 1980), 152

217 F Groome, *Ordnance Gazetteer* (Glasgow, 1894–95), Wigtownshire

218 The earls' main property in the parish was at Rispain, south-west of the
burgh; see *A Directory of Landownership in Scotland c 1770*, ed L R Timperley
(Scottish Record Society, 1976), 350

219 To found a new village close to his new house was standard practice for an
improving landowner. As a port it may have been designed to take trade
away from Wigtown more than Isle of Whithorn. For a recent discussion, see
L J Philip, 'Planned villages in Dumfries and Galloway 1730–1850', *Scottish
Geographical Journal* 119.2 (2003), 77–98

220 Webster, *Agriculture of Galloway*, 17, 37

221 *OSA*, 535–6, 539

222 Webster, *Agriculture of Galloway*, 4–5. Selkirk's property was at St Mary's Isle,
south of Kirkcudbright

223 *OSA* Glasserton, 396–7; also imported lime and coal

224 *OSA*, 548

225 *Ibid*; Campbell, *Owners and Occupiers*, 6, when coal duty was removed in 1793,
the Cumberland coalmasters put their prices up, so Galloway did not benefit
much

226 *OSA*, 549

227 Samuel Smith, *General View of the Agriculture of Galloway* (London, 1810),
330–1

228 Pococke, *Tour through Scotland, 1760*, ed D W Kemp (SHS, Edinburgh, 1887),
17

229 Webster, *Agriculture of Galloway*, 14

230 Oram, *Whithorn and Monastic Estate Management*, 7, 11, 16

231 I Donnachie, 'The Economy of Galloway in Historical Perspective', in *The Galloway Project: a Study of the Economy of South West Scotland with Particular Reference to its Tourist Potential* (Scottish Tourist Board, Edinburgh, 1968), 6.10–6.11

232 Webster, *Agriculture of Galloway*, 14

233 Smith, *Agriculture of Galloway*, 329

234 Webster, *Agriculture of Galloway*, 14

235 Smith, *Agriculture of Galloway*, 353

236 *OSA*, 551

237 *Ibid*; for more about the tanning industry, see I Donnachie, *The Industrial Archaeology of Galloway* (Newton Abbot, 1971), 45–50

238 Donnachie, *Industrial Archaeology*, 55

239 Donnachie, *Industrial Archaeology*, 41; the print is in the Priory Museum

240 *Dumfries and Galloway Through the Lens, 16, Glimpses of old Whithorn and Glasserton Parishes* (Dumfries, 1999), 23

241 NAS RHP42253; NAS GD10/221, another mill is documented at Broughton at the north end of the parish in 1738

242 Donnachie, *Industrial Archaeology*, 153

243 Quotation from initial survey, in Campbell, *Owners and Occupiers*, 7

244 W Taylor, *The Military Roads in Scotland* (Newton Abbot, 1976), 100

245 Webster, *Agriculture of Galloway*, 20; Donnachie, *Industrial Archaeology*, 26; Taylor, *Military Roads*, 100–1, 111, the Road Trustees took over responsibility for the military road in 1807

246 Smith, *Agriculture of Galloway*, 317

247 *The Book of Galloway 1745*, reprinted from the *Galloway Gazette* (Newton Stewart, 1912), 67

248 Pococke, *Tour*, 17

249 *OSA*, 58

250 *Ordnance Gazetteer*

251 *OSA* 542, 550. The importance of the Customs presence to a small community is highlighted by the survival of the wills of a Surveyor of Customs (1725), a Commander of HM Cutter (1799), and the relict of an Excise Officer (1806), NAS CC8/8/90, CC22/3/4B, CC22/3/5A

252 MacLeod, *Discovering Galloway*, 225

253 For medieval fishing activities, see Oram, *Whithorn and Monastic Estate Management*, 13–15

254 NAS RHP 42253. No definite trace of it remains, though there are many boulders in that area of the foreshore which may have formed part of it

255 Ralegh Radford, 'Whithorn: Final Report'

256 *OSA*, 544

257 *Dumfries and Galloway Through the Lens, 16*, 20, has a photograph of the building, which was replaced in 1892 by the United Presbyterian Church, now a garage

258 *OSA* 547

259 *CRB*, iv, 301, 463, 492

260 NAS GD18/2215

261 Pococke, *Tour*, 17; the assumption is that it was whitened as a daymark for shipping, though it is not clear how widely it would have been visible

262 Gifford, *Dumfries and Galloway*, 567–8. RCAHMS, *Tolbooths and Townhouses*, 199–200, regards the present tower and spire as dating from the early 19th century, though the 'carefully-wrought ashlar of its conical spire may have been reused'

263 RCAHMS, *Tolbooths and Townhouses*, 200. In 1994 the spire was struck by lightening and the bell fell. It is now in the Visitor Centre

264 *Book of Galloway 1745*, 67

265 *OSA*, 533

266 G A Cooke, *Topographical Description of Scotland*, Southern Scotland (London, *c* 1805), 238

267 Pococke, *Tour*, 17–18

268 NAS RHP663, 'Plan of the orchard of Isle of Whithorn', 1780

269 NAS RHP42253, 'The Harbour of Whithorn', 1818

270 NAS GD455/53

271 M'Kerlie, *Lands and their Owners*, 421

272 *OSA*, 547

273 *OSA vol. 1, General*, 144–8, 'Population of the Towns of Scotland, containing 300 Souls and upwards'

274 *OSA*, 551

275 *Dumfries Weekly Journal*, 10 February 1801, report of a dinner

276 Consolidated Taxes, NAS E326/15/31

277 See, for example, R D Oram, 'Torhousemuir Historical Account. Report on A Programme of Research Undertaken by Retrospect Historical Services on Behalf of Scottish Natural Heritage' (1995), for an analysis of the immigration process and its impact

278 *Pigot and Co's New Commercial Directory of Scotland for 1825–26* (London and Manchester)

279 *Report upon the boundaries of the several cities burghs and towns of Scotland … 1832*

280 *Poor Law Inquiry Commission for Scotland* (1844), Examinations, Synod of Galloway, Parish of Whithorn, 529, the minister dated the need for regular voluntary contributions from the heritors for the maintenance of the poor as starting from a bad harvest in 1826

281 *OSA* 540–1, 'There is a very promising appearance of a Copper mine, near the Isle of Whithorn, which has hitherto been totally neglected'; *NSA*, 53–4, 'Trial has been repeatedly made for coal, but hitherto without success. Upon the estate of Tonderghie, close by the shore, a mining company … sunk a shaft to a considerable depth in quest of copper, and succeeded in discovering a small scattered vein, and procured a few very rich specimens of ore. The attempt was discontinued at a time when every interest in the country was involved in general distress'; Cooke, *Topographical Description of Scotland*, 238, 'specimens of lead and copper are found here, and slate of a good quality, but neither are wrought to any extent'; *Ordnance Gazetteer*, 'At Tonderghie, S of Whithorn, there is a vein of barytes associated with iron and copper pyrites'.

For the Tonderghie mine see Donnachie, *Industrial Archaeology*, 127, 230; Hugh Stewart of Tonderghie was an improving landlord

282 *Pigot's Directory, 1825*

283 *OSA*, 282

284 MacLeod, *Discovering Galloway*, 223

285 *NSA*, 53

286 MacLeod, *Discovering Galloway*, 223

287 *Ordnance Gazetteer*

288 J Cannon, *Droll Recollections of Whithorn and Vicinity* (Dumfries, 1904), 28; western Galloway is not a very big area, and the fairs never seem to have been large

289 *Ordnance Gazetteer*

290 Evidence from *Trade Directories*

291 *Ordnance Gazetteer*

292 It is not listed in *Pigot's Directory, 1837*, but is marked on the 1st edition OS map of 1849. It may have been one of the seven branches of the short-lived Southern Bank of Scotland (established 1838), based in Dumfries, which was taken over by the Edinburgh and Glasgow Bank in 1841 (S G Checkland, *Scottish Banking: a history 1695–1973* (Glasgow & London, 1975), 340)

293 C W Munn, *Clydesdale Bank: the first hundred years* (London and Glasgow, 1988), 69

294 It is marked on the 1849 OS map at roughly 48 George Street, close to the Ket burn. In 1958 the National merged with the Commercial, and later was taken over by the Royal Bank

295 *NSA*, 59; the savings bank was part of a national movement to encourage the lower classes to save, and was not the same as a commercial bank

296 *Ordnance Gazetteer*

297 M M Harper, *Rambles in Galloway*, 3rd edn (Dumfries, 1908), 411

298 *NSA*, 54

299 *Ordnance Gazetteer*

300 Harper, *Rambles in Galloway*, 411

301 The Company was later taken over by the county council

302 *Third Statistical Account of Scotland, The County of Wigtown*, M C Arnott (ed) (Glasgow, 1965), parish of Whithorn, Rev John Scoular, 1952 and 1962, 423; *Dumfries and Galloway Through the Lens, 18, Glimpses of old Galloway Seaports* (Dumfries, 2000), 6; the remains of the retaining wall of the pond can still be seen

303 Donnachie, *Industrial Archaeology*, 31, 203; *Ordnance Gazetteer*

304 *NSA*, 58

305 *NSA*, 57–8

306 *Ordnance Gazetteer*, Wigtownshire

307 Campbell, *Owners and Occupiers*, 9. It was the advent of steam shipping which moved the Irish route from Port William and Port Patrick to Stranraer

308 *Dumfries and Galloway Through the Lens, 18*, includes photographs of oyster smacks, a paddle steamer and the lifeboat at the Isle; *Slater's Directories, 1837–89*

309   Donnachie, 'The Economy', fig 6.1; Campbell, *Owners and Occupiers*, 26

310   M'Kerlie, *Lands and their Owners*, 420

311   *Third Statistical Account*, 423

312   C H Dick, *Highways and Byways in Galloway and Carrick*, London, 1916

313   J Morris, *An Illustrated Guide to our Lifeboat Stations, 7, Scotland* (privately
       published, nd), 2–3; *Dumfries and Galloway Through the Lens, 16, 33*, there were
       three boats in succession, but they were replaced by a motor boat based at
       Kirkcudbright in 1920. The ruins of the lifeboat house have been tidied up
       and now contain the pile of stones brought by pilgrims to the chapel

314   D L Smith, *The Little Railways of South-West Scotland* (Newton Abbot, 1969),
       86–98

315   Donnachie, *Industrial Archaeology*, 191–4 with map of railway network in
       Galloway

316   *Official Guide to the Royal Burgh of Whithorn issued by authority of Whithorn
       Town Council* (Newton Stewart, *c* 1950), 14

317   *NSA*, 53

318   Dick, *Highways and Byways of Galloway*, vii

319   *Slater's Directory, 1911*

320   Cannon, *Droll Recollections*; *Slater's Directories*

321   Gifford, *Dumfries and Galloway*, 567; *Ordnance Gazetteer*

322   *Pigot's Directory, 1825*. The minister in the *NSA* also praised it and its situation

323   M'Kerlie, *Lands and their Owners*, 435

324   Pococke, *Tour*, 15

325   M'Kerlie, *Lands and their Owners*, 435

326   Gifford, *Dumfries and Galloway*, 567

327   *NSA*, 58

328   *Dumfries and Galloway Through the Lens, 16*, 22, the access was made this way
       to avoid any damage to potential archaeological remains closer to the priory

329   *Pigot's Directory, 1825*

330   Gifford, *Dumfries and Galloway*, 567

331   This is because the town did not own the Isle, only the harbour. Presumably
       no landowner offered land to build a church, so the town offered what
       it could, demonstrating its support for the new Free Church. Half the
       Isle lay within the lands of Drummaston, the other half appears to have
       belonged originally to the barony of Cutreoch, owned by the Houston
       family. Cutreoch, Morrach and the 'mill of Bysbie', immediately across the
       Drummullin Burn from the Castle at the Isle, had been in the possession of
       the Houston family from at least 1545, when Michael Houston in Cutcloy
       was given sasine by Adam Blackadder, commendator of Dundrennan
       (GD455/15/5). The lands of Bysbie, the core of the later Dundrennan barony
       of the Morrach, had been in the possession of the abbey since before 1305
       (Bain, *Cal of Documents rel to Scotland*, ii, 1884, no. 1702). For landownership
       in the parish of Whithorn in the later 18th century, see *Directory of
       Landownership*, 350. Both properties changed hands in the later eighteenth
       century and by 1818, the burn marked the boundary between the half of the
       Isle possessed by the laird of Physgill, and the lands of Boyach, possessed by

the laird of Tonderghie (NAS RHP44253)

332   Gifford, *Dumfries and Galloway*, 567

333   *Ordnance Gazetteer*, 1895; *Dumfries and Galloway Through the Lens, 16,* 21. Bute had bought High Mains from the Earl of Galloway

334   R McCluskey, 'Introduction: celebrating St Ninian', in McCluskey (ed), *The See of Ninian: A History of the Medieval Diocese of Whithorn and the Diocese of Galloway in Modern Times* (Ayr, 1997), 12–14

335   B Aspinwall, 'The Making of the Modern Diocese of Galloway', in R McCluskey (ed), *See of Ninian*, 177. The canons left in 1897.

336   *Report on Municipal Corporations*, 429, the gaoler was away at the harvest when the inspector came, and refused to return, so 'the Reporter could not get access to a low apartment, or vault, in which a maniac is confined for life, under sentence of the High court of Justiciary, for killing a man; the person sent to officiate for the gaoler broke the key in endeavouring to open the door; but in so far as any opinion could be formed, from its external appearance, the vault was of the worst description'

337   *Ordnance Gazetteer*, 1895; Gifford, *Dumfries and Galloway*, 567. David Henry's only other work outside Fife was remodelling Glasserton parish church in 1891 (online Dictionary of Scottish Architects). Perhaps the link between Whithorn and St Andrews was the Marquess of Bute

338   *Dumfries and Galloway Through the Lens, 16,* 6

339   Gifford, *Dumfries and Galloway*, 567

340   *NSA*, 58–9; *Poor Law Inquiry (1844)*, 529, 'The kirk session recommend such poor children as they think proper, to the parochial schoolmasters, who educate them gratis. Lady Galloway has a free school, where fifty girls, between the ages of six and twelve, are educated'

341   Gifford, *Dumfries and Galloway*, 568; *Third Statistical Account*, 424; *Slater's Directory, 1915*

342   *NSA*, 54

343   Harper, *Rambles in Galloway*, 410

344   *Dumfries and Galloway Through the Lens, 2, Glimpses of Old Whithorn* (Dumfries, 1997), 7, the building is now the Visitor Centre

345   *Dumfries and Galloway Through the Lens, 16,* 38–9

346   *Third Statistical Account*, 425

347   *Third Statistical Account*, 425; *Dumfries and Galloway Through the Lens, 16,* 42, part of the cost was also raised by some 'Liverpool gentlemen'

348   *Dumfries and Galloway Through the Lens, 16,* 7, and recent local information

349   *Dumfries and Galloway Through the Lens, 16,* 43

350   Harper, *Rambles in Galloway*, 411

351   NAS SC19/41/7 and 19/41/12

352   *Pigot's Directory, 1825*

353   *Ordnance Gazetteer*, Isle of Whithorn

354   G Clark, 'Rural Land Use from *c.*1870', in Whittington and Whyte, *An Historical Geography of Scotland* (London, 1983), 229

355   Extracted from data downloaded from website <u>ScotlandsPeople.gov.uk</u>

356   NAS SC19/41/12, 1866, David McConnell, master of the ship *Fulwood* of

Liverpool, residing at Isle of Whithorn; SC 19/41/19, 1893, John Webster, sometime captain of *Bellisle* of Liverpool, residing in Whithorn, latterly residing in Newton Stewart; SC19/41/14, 1873, Peter Whannel, residing in Liverpool or elsewhere in Lancashire, thereafter at Whithorn; SC19/41/14, 1875, Francis Carlyle Broadfoot, dockmaster, residing in Liverpool, thereafter in Whithorn; SC19/41/16, 1881, Agnes Dinnel (Brodie), widow of William Dinnel, master mariner, Isle of Whithorn, died at Liverpool

357 NAS SC19/41/1, William Martin, SC19/41//18, William Fiddes, SC19/41/22, Samuel Stroyan, SC19/41/20, Robert Fleming

358 NAS SC19/41/18, 1887 William Thorburn, master mariner, Isle, died at Whitehaven, Cumberland; SC19/41/19, 1890 Catherine Lockhart, widow of George Lockhart, blacksmith, sometime residing in Whitehaven, afterwards in Whithorn

359 Birchman, Old Kirkyard

360 *NSA*, 60

361 J E Handley, *The Irish in Scotland, 1798–1845* (Cork, 1945), 216; *Poor Law Inquiry,* 529, 'the paupers are either Irish or descended from the Irish'

362 Campbell, *Owners and Occupiers,* 37

363 T M Devine, *The Scottish Nation* (London, 1999), 503–4

364 G Walker, The Protestant Irish in Scotland', in T M Devine (ed), *Irish Immigrants and Scottish Society in the Nineteenth and Twentieth Centuries* (Edinburgh, 1991), 48–50; *Report from Select Committee on Orange Institutions in Great Britain and the Colonies* (1835), Report, 24, appendix 19, 143, Whithorn was Lodge no. 127

365 Campbell, *Owners and Occupiers,* 8

366 Campbell, *Owners and Occupiers,* 36. Those who could afford it chose to emigrate to America

367 Faed and Sloan, *Galloway,* 222

368 *Dumfries and Galloway Through the Lens, 16,* 5

369 *Third Statistical Account,* 422

370 NMRS site NX43SE 4; *Third Statistical Account,* 423; D Thomson, *226 heavy anti-aircraft battery 1939–1945: a personal account of the Caithness and Orkney battery* (Kirkwall, 1995), 3

371 *Third Statistical Account,* 423; J Evans, E Palmer and R Walter (eds), *A Harbour Goes to War: the story of Mulberry and the men who made it happen* (Garlieston, c.2000); A T Murchie, *The Mulberry Harbour Project in Wigtownshire in 1942–1944* (Wigtown, 1993)

372 *Third Statistical Account,* 424. This is reinforced by recent oral testimony that this was done to avoid living in tied housing, and the result was a network of footpaths leading out to the surrounding farms

373 *Official Guide to Whithorn,* 13

374 *Third Statistical Account,* 425; *Dumfries and Galloway Through the Lens, 16,* 5

375 *Third Statistical Account,* 425

376 *Third Statistical Account,* 368

377 *Third Statistical Account,* 424

378 *Third Statistical Account,* 368

379 Donnachie, 'Economy of Galloway', 6.5

380 *Third Statistical Account*, 365; local oral testimony

381 Hill, *Whithorn*, 276, one of the early greenhouses was excavated by the Whithorn Trust

382 MacLeod, *Discovering Galloway*, 221

383 Local oral testimony

384 *Third Statistical Account*, 360

385 Morris, *Lifeboat Stations*, 2–3

386 *Third Statistical Account*, 422

387 *Official Guide to Whithorn*, 16

388 *Official Guide to Whithorn*, 26

389 *Official Guide to Whithorn*, 15

390 *Romantic Galloway. Guide and Holiday Brochure for South West Scotland* (Castle Douglas, 1954)

391 *Official Guide to Whithorn*

392 A Scoular, 'Tourism in the Whithorn area of South West Scotland' (unpublished undergraduate dissertation, Dept of Geography, University of St Andrews, 1994), the excavations attracted 15,232 visitors in 1992; over 75% of his sample came from England; and only 16% came to the area for its history

393 *Official Guide to Whithorn*, 26

394 MacLeod, *Exploring Galloway*, 225

395 Aspinwall, 'The Making of the Modern Diocese of Galloway', 179–80

396 McCluskey, 'Introduction', 14–20

397 Gifford, *Dumfries and Galloway*, 567. Plans had been drawn up by Basil Spence for a much larger pilgrimage church, but were not used

398 *Dumfries and Galloway Through the Lens*, 16, 21

4: The Potential of Whithorn (maps 10 & 11)

The ruins of such an important pilgrimage site have attracted the attention of archaeologists for well over 150 years, and will continue to do so (**fig 36**). However, the focus on the priory has eclipsed study of the burgh, and the crucial relationships between the two are not fully understood. Equally, the relationship between Whithorn and its port, some two and a half miles away at Isle of Whithorn, does not appear to have been fully explored. This section, therefore, will examine the burgh and its port in the following sequence: the setting; George Street (the focus of pilgrimage), the upper town, and the lower town; dating the fabric; suburban expansion and rigs; recent change; and Isle of Whithorn. This is followed by suggestions for further research.

Whithorn shelters in a fold in the plateau of southern Galloway not far from the tip of the peninsula. It comprises an exceptionally spacious market-place, the upper section sloping northwards down a ridge between low marshy ground to the north-west, and ground sloping to the south-east. It is narrowed at the top (south) by the High Port Mouth and at the northern end by Low Port Mouth, these narrowings having survived threats of removal during the twentieth century. While the urban form clearly indicates that these were the original locations for town gates, there is no evidence that Whithorn was ever fortified or needed to be; in that respect it conforms to the Scottish norm. The town gates did, however, have other functions, such as control of admissions and the collection of customs. Extensive suburbs extend farther out on each side.

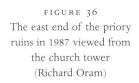

FIGURE 36
The east end of the priory ruins in 1987 viewed from the church tower
(Richard Oram)

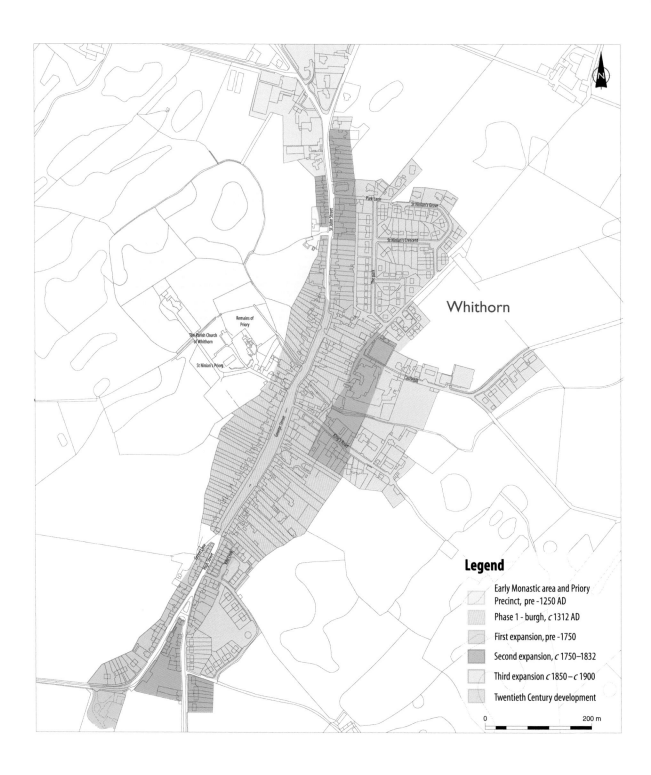

Whithorn

Legend

Early Monastic area and Priory
Precinct, pre -1250 AD

Phase 1 - burgh, *c* 1312 AD

First expansion, pre -1750

Second expansion, *c* 1750–1832

Third expansion *c* 1850 – *c* 1900

Twentieth Century development

0   200 m

MAP 10
Whithorn development map

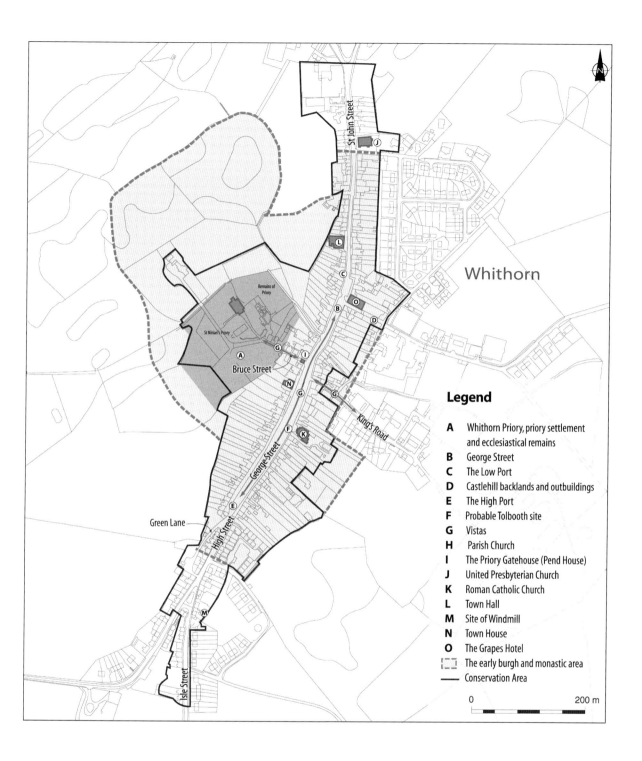

Whithorn

Legend

A   Whithorn Priory, priory settlement
     and ecclesiastical remains
B   George Street
C   The Low Port
D   Castlehill backlands and outbuildings
E   The High Port
F   Probable Tolbooth site
G   Vistas
H   Parish Church
I   The Priory Gatehouse (Pend House)
J   United Presbyterian Church
K   Roman Catholic Church
L   Town Hall
M   Site of Windmill
N   Town House
O   The Grapes Hotel
    The early burgh and monastic area
    Conservation Area

0   200 m

MAP II
Whithorn character map

Possible stone wall-footings were identified in a cable-trench cut along the middle of George Street, in line with the entrance to St Ninian's Roman Catholic Church. It seems likely that these mark the site of the pre-1814 tolbooth, and indeed the location matches that on Roy's map (**map 3**).[1] Just how large the tolbooth was is unclear: Roy's map of *c* 1750 shows a square building of reasonable size, while Bishop Pococke refers to a well-whitened square tower in the middle of the street, but also to a 'market house'. It is likely that these were two parts of the same building, and the latter was a fine structure judging from its description as 'adorned with spire and turrets and prouded with bells'.[2] It stood at the widest part of the street, with its rear coinciding with where the street alignment changes sharply – rather as was the case in St Andrews. In this uphill section between the rear of the tolbooth and the High Port (or Isle Port Mouth), houses on the north-west side are set back substantially, and still have forelands (privately owned land between the houses and the public pavement). In rural European towns, and small Scottish ones, that is where one would expect dung heaps, each with its own retaining wall; that this was also the case in Whithorn is confirmed by a local rhyme:

Whithorn is a pleasant town,
A Tolbooth with a steeple;
A wee dunghill at every door,
And full of Irish people.

The downhill section of the market-place, between the facade of the tolbooth and the Ket burn, was probably Whithorn's principal ceremonial area. Here was the market cross, and it was here that the principal pilgrimage routes by sea and land converged at the stately gatehouse to the priory.

Until the mid-nineteenth century, the Ket burn, crossed by a 'good bridge',[3] ran across the market-place itself in a south-easterly direction

FIGURE 37
Low Port Mouth, where
the street narrows at the
north end of George Street
(Richard Oram)

FIGURE 38
A fireplace of hand-made bricks inserted
into an earlier stone building at the
back of a rig on the east side of George
Street (Paula Martin)

FIGURE 39
The road along the back of
the rigs of the northern part
of the east side of George
Street (Paula Martin)

from the priory precinct – thus effectively acting as a space-divider. To the
south-east of George Street, an industrial suburb in the neighbourhood of
the Ket burn, with tannery and shambles (slaughterhouse), had emerged by
the later eighteenth century. It is the area where one would expect to find
such industries, with power and flushing provided by the burn. Across the
Ket to the north, George Street widens again into a square, immediately
before being narrowed by Low Port Mouth (**fig 37**). This 'square' was the
location of at least two inns. Today, so far as can be ascertained, it has some
of the oldest structures in Whithorn. This is where carts and carriages
would have entered from the north, and it is reasonable to suppose that
it was the town's service centre – a miniature equivalent of Edinburgh's
Grassmarket.

Perhaps deceived by a rocky outcrop, a castle site was identified on the
earliest Ordnance Survey maps, on a raised knoll to the north-east of the
town (now in the public park). There is no evidence of a castle at this
location, and the established late medieval episcopal 'castle' site was at the
bishop's property of Balnespick or Bishopton, to the north-west of the
priory precinct. A more appropriate location to search for a defensive site
might be the semicircular raised area bounded by a burn and marsh lying
north-west of the priory. However, the back rigs of Whithorn are developed

for work only in this single location to the north-east, where there appears to have been a later loan (lane) running alongside 'Castlehill' (see **map 11**). This was possibly for taking the burgh's cattle out to the rather limited common lands represented by the farm called 'Common Park'. The loan may originally have extended south-west, through a ford across the Ket burn, to enter the town along Rotten Row, although the road to Portyerrock existed by the time of General Roy's map. The rigs in this part of town have all been developed with buildings which, to judge from fireplaces and other evidence, may have been smithies, stables, and the like (**fig 38**). Although all are now largely derelict, there is considerable townscape and historical value in this sector (**fig 39**).

Whithorn's enormous market-place seems divisible into three portions: the ceremonial section and main market area at the centre, facing the tolbooth and the priory gatehouse, where one might expect to find the most important structures; the upper town behind the tolbooth, where the houses are set back; and the commercial area across the Ket burn to the north. It is possible that Whithorn was laid out on a grander scale than its economy was able to support. But the evidence suggests that the town was fully occupied in its heyday prior to 1650, and to a scale and quality that related to the substantial cathedral-priory. That appears confirmed by Andrew Symson who, writing shortly after 1684, stated 'of old, it was a town of great trade, and resort' (resort referring, presumably, to the pilgrims).[4] The three divisions of the market-place are proposed to make sense of an otherwise over-ambitious space, and may provide a guide to what to look for within the surviving structures.

The suburbs

To the south (uphill) lies the suburb once named West Port, renamed High Street before 1894 (**fig 40**), which divides into roads running south to Isle of Whithorn and south-west to Glasserton. There is nothing marked in this area on Roy's map of c 1750 (**map 3**), but it was developed by the time of the 1832 boundary map (**map 7**). It may have evolved with a triangular green at the centre.[5] It was clearly the first point of delivery for anything arriving for the town by sea. It was the location of the town's windmill and seed store, and was, within living memory, a part of town colonised by Irish immigrants, many of whom became craft-workers and tradesmen, or carried out jobs such as ditching and dyking. Its pub, the Calcutta, was established c 1880 (**fig 41**).[6]

To the north there was little if any development before c 1750, but expansion was achieved and most building plots occupied by 1832. The rigs extending along St John Street beyond Low Port Mouth imply sporadic suburban development along the north-west side (working round three pre-

FIGURE 40
Whithorn High Street,
1962 (Crown copyright:
RCAHMS)

FIGURE 41
The Calcutta Inn and a
Glenfield and Kennedy
water pump, High Street,
Whithorn, 1962 (RCAHMS)
(Crown copyright:
RCAHMS)

existing houses); but the regular rigs on the opposite side imply that these cottages were laid out all at one time, probably in the late eighteenth or early nineteenth century. In the later nineteenth century, particularly after the arrival of the railway, it seems that the commercial focus of the town may have moved north, reinforced by the establishment of the creamery next to the station in 1902.

Focus of pilgrimage

The priory, shrine to St Ninian, and cathedral lay to the north-west of the burgh on a raised plateau once almost entirely surrounded by the marsh and meadows around the Ket burn. The church was longer than any other Premonstratensian church in Scotland,[7] and its associated burgh was likewise unmatched in scale by any other of its kind. The priory was the chief *raison d'être* of Whithorn and the prior was the burgh's superior, but it was pilgrims to the shrine of St Ninian who probably provided Whithorn with its principal source of income. One may assume that, as in Tain, Whithorn did very well commercially from being a significant pilgrimage destination – by way of taverns and hostelries, inns and stables, and souvenir-peddlers. Almost certainly the priory was responsible for the handsome canalising and stone revetting of the Ket burn as it passed through priory property (**fig 42**), since it would have had the effect of draining the ground to make more land available for priory activity, as well as securing a steady flow of water to flush the monastic latrines and kitchen drains.

That the priory lands were fully delineated *before* the establishment of the burgh and the laying out of its rigs is indicated by the distorted angle of, for example, no. 29 George Street, which lies at an angle in order to dovetail with the priory boundary (**fig 43**). The precinct was reached from the burgh via the priory gatehouse (**fig 44**), no. 53 George Street, and up what is now Bruce Street. The excavated evidence for what appear to have been traders' booths in the Glebe Field, together with the sequence of offerings made by James IV during his pilgrimages, suggests that pilgrims were directed towards the west end of the priory church, probably entering through the nave. Given the internal arrangement of other medieval monastic precincts in Scotland, it is likely that most traffic was directed round the west end of the church, roughly along the line of the existing Bruce Street, towards the cloister and main ancillary complex which lay to the north. The positioning of the 'commendator's house', the site of which is partly overlain by the line of Bruce Street leading round to the nineteenth-century manse, indicates that the road west of the churchyard gate, field wall and churchyard boundary wall as laid out currently are all probably of nineteenth-century date.

Pilgrims could enter the town along four pilgrimage routes. Those who came by sea to Isle of Whithorn harbour could have approached the town by a footpath which ended in Rotten Row (King's Road), debouching into the burgh's principal ceremonial part at a point evenly placed between the tolbooth and the priory gatehouse. As pilgrims drew near, the route was probably focused axially upon a presumed tower at the priory. Pilgrims going to or from St Ninian's Cave would enter or leave the town through High or Isle Port Mouth. Pilgrims might also arrive at the same point if coming through Glasserton from Ayrshire and the north-west, and enter the town

FIGURE 42 (left)
A section of the canalised Ket burn near the priory (Richard Oram)

FIGURE 43 (above)
The backs of two properties in George Street showing a change of
alignment of the back rigs (Paula Martin)

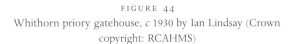

FIGURE 44
Whithorn priory gatehouse, c 1930 by Ian Lindsay (Crown
copyright: RCAHMS)

from the top of the hill; or they might enter the town from Wigtown and the north-east through the suburb that straggled along St John Street. The row of cottages in Glasserton still called 'Beggars' Row,' however, is more likely to refer to seasonal workers than to medieval pilgrims.

Today the scale of the priory church is considerably diminished by a number of factors which makes appreciation of it almost impossible. The principal survival above ground is a section of the nave, which was truncated at the west end in the early eighteenth century when its tower collapsed. To make matters worse, its floor level was raised by over a metre and its wall-heads lowered after it ceased to be a cathedral in 1688–90. Its current two splendid doors were rescued from elsewhere in the priory and reset here to adorn what must have been a fairly plain nave during its refitting as the cathedral for the revived Episcopalian diocese in the early seventeenth century. The raised floor not only reduces its apparent height but conceals the mural tombs from adequate inspection and appreciation (**fig 45**). That diminution is exacerbated by the ground around its south-west corner having been significantly raised by the debris from the collapsed tower, which appears never to have been removed but left simply to grass over. Worst, perhaps, is the way the path to the 1822 parish church, located on the site of the east range of the cloister and the reredorter, cuts through the crossing of the priory church, rendering the entire structure much smaller and less significant than it once clearly was. Cutting the church into two in this fashion destroys all sense of the original scale.

There is considerable scope for more excavation in the neighbourhood of the priory, particularly where the ground rises at the west end of the church, and where the current footpath cuts across the priory toward the parish church. If new excavations are carried out in the area of the crossing, the opportunity should be taken to reroute access to the parish church, so that the priory church might be presented as an entity.

Pilgrimage destinations in Scotland usually signalled their presence by towers. Tall, slim campaniles adorned Balmerino Abbey and possibly St Duthac's shrine at Tain, as a guide to visitors. Whithorn Priory, a considerably more important location than either of these, was likely to have had such a tower that would be visible to pilgrims not just from a distance, but also as they approached along the winding St John Street or up Rotten Row. Given the likely height of the priory church of *c* 20m at least, a tower in suitable proportion would be unlikely to be much less than 30m high. It would be difficult to exaggerate the presence such an enormous building would have exerted over its burgh, a presence enhanced by the fact that the plinth on which it was built was already significantly elevated about street level. One

FIGURE 45
The top of a mural tomb recess demonstrates how much the floor of the priory church has been raised (Colin Martin)

function of such a priory tower or campanile would have been to house bells to summon pilgrims to the shrine when it was not being used for normal priory devotions. This could imply that there might have been a pilgrim gathering area, perhaps between the Ket burn and the tolbooth.

Archaeological investigations in the town (map 12)

There have been few excavations within the burgh, and these have not found evidence of its medieval origins. Excavations to the rear of no. 62 George Street following the demolition of some sheds revealed a stone-lined well, and from under the floor of the house, building work recovered a collection of eighteenth- or nineteenth-century artefacts and a sequence of earlier clay floors. Similar finds, along with the remains of a wall and floor of an earlier building, were recovered during work on the south side of King's Road.[8] Some millstones, recorded as being found in the floor of one of the sheds at no. 62 George Street, appear in fact to have come from the former cinema.[9] They, like the remains of the building, are undated and could potentially be medieval, though they are probably later, and may have come from the windmill at the top of the town. A pit found in the living room of no. 117 George Street also produced eighteenth- or nineteenth-century finds. Building work at nos 30–32 George Street allowed for an archaeological inspection of foundation trenches. The land to the rear of the property was 1m higher than that on which the house was built and suggests that topsoil has been imported in this area of the town; no archaeological remains were identified as a result. A similar finding, of made-up ground to the rear of the property, was made at no. 51 George Street, on the opposite side of the road.[10] A watching brief to the rear of no. 73 George Street found that garden soil to a depth of 0.68m overlay clay subsoil and natural greywacke bedrock.[11]

Dating the fabric

Whithorn presents a number of difficulties in dating its fabric. First, greywacke stone produces such a different building form to sandstone or granite that the typical methods of studying wall thickness elsewhere in Scotland do not work well. Moreover, it shares with granite an exemption from weathering. In addition, many of the more recent details and roofing practices appear more English than Scottish. Nonetheless, some general points can be made.

At first glance, the town seems to present a predominantly nineteenth-century appearance, coinciding with the period between the maps of c 1750 and 1832 when the town expanded beyond its medieval boundary, and the period between c 1840 and c 1880 when the town was at its most prosperous and populous, based on maritime trade through the Isle. Where the List of Buildings of Architectural or Historic Interest can ascertain no fixed date

Whithorn

Legend

▼ Archaeological Interventions

● Museum

★ Archaeological Findspot

0   200m

MAP 12
Whithorn archaeological finds map (left)

No.	Name	NGR	NMRS
	Archaeological interventions		
1	Whithorn Priory – A programme of archaeological work was undertaken to explore the boundaries of the ecclesiastical settlement. Excavation revealed evidence for rig and furrow cultivation, a rough stone surface associated with industrial activity, and a possible fenced or palisaded enclosure. Remote sensing surveys over an area of ground at the E end of Whithorn Priory Cathedral showed the remains of what may be the S wall of the choir and a S stair down to the crypt.	NX 443 403	NX44SW 5 NX44SW 48 NX44SW 81
2	Whithorn Priory – Eight trenches were excavated along a 450m N–S line in the fields SW of Whithorn Priory. No significant archaeological remains were revealed.	NX 4431 4033 - NX 4433 3989	
3	Bruce Street – A small-scale evaluation was undertaken in the SE corner of Fey Field, to the SW of the Priory. The principal aim of the evaluation was to investigate the nature of a large rectilinear resistance anomaly which had been identified during the course of earlier geophysical surveys. Topsoil stripping revealed the outline of a robbed building, coincident with the geophysical anomaly, and several cut features, probably graves. Intrusive excavation of these features lay outwith the brief and the trenches were backfilled upon completion.	NX 4441 4027	NX44SW 79
4	The Pend and 53 George Street – The removal of blocking windows in the room above The Pend and removal of wet-dash render on the exterior N side of The Pend provided an opportunity to study its development. An originally late-medieval structure, interpreted as a gatehouse with a building attached on the N side entered from within The Pend, it was substantially rebuilt in the post-medieval period. There are indications that the original building may have lain at right angles to the street and that The Pend may have originally been covered with a barrel vault.	NX 445 402	NX44SW 58
5	George Street – Five holes were excavated up to 1.6m deep. The first (A) revealed demolition rubble consisting of mixed local greywacke stone, mid-grey Cumbrian slate roof tiles and unglazed floor tiles. Below this was a floor deposit which overlay a mixed deposit containing charcoal and fragments of burnt bone, possibly evidence of the medieval graveyard. The second (B) was sited on the location of a previous telegraph pole. Below this, five fragments of bone were revealed, possibly indicative of the 6th–10th century graveyard identified in excavation seasons of 1995–96. The third (C) revealed the foundations of the existing boundary wall with 61 George Street with a large number of 18th- and 19th-century finds uncovered, mainly pottery and glass sherds. The fourth (D) contained two sherds of modern pottery and bedrock. The fifth (E) contained no archaeological remains and bedrock was encountered.	NX 444 403	
6	30–32 George Street – An archaeological watching brief was carried out during the excavation of foundation trenches for an extension to the rear of 30–32 George Street. No archaeoloogical deposits were revealed.	NX 446 402	NX44SW 57.01
7	62 George Street – An archaeological watching brief was carried out during the demolition of the wall column between the W ground-floor window and the S doorway of 62 George Street. A carved gravestone cross-slab, depicting scenes of possible Christian art with human and animal figures, was revealed. It dated from the 10th to 11th century AD and had later been re-used as a door lintel.	NX 4457 4018	NX44SW 50
8	51 George Street – An archaeological watching brief was carried out following the removal of internal floor deposits. A level of made ground was revealed beneath the floor surface, but no finds or structures were noted in the exposed levels. A number of boulders underlay the rear wall of the building which may be part of the foundations of an earlier wall line.	NX 44551 40256	
9	68 St John Street – Foundation trenches for an extension were excavated. No archaeological remains were revealed.	NX 4464 4040	

No.	Name	NGR	NMRS
10	62 George Street – An early yellow-mortared, stone-lined well covered by a stone slab was found below the quarry-tiled floor of the W shed joined with the back of the house. There were no finds from below the concrete and quarry-tiled floors of the sheds, which may have had earth floors and thatched roofs originally. The underfloor rubble layers above the natural red clay in each of the ground-floor rooms of the house were excavated by the builders to a lower depth, producing a collection of 18th- to 19th-century wine-bottle glass, domestic pottery, a bone baby spoon and a silver coin of George III (c 1816–18). Earlier clay floor layers were found in the section of the builders' wall trench below the floor of the middle room of the house, though there was no evidence of earlier occupation below these clay floor surfaces.	NX 4457 4018	NX44SW 53.00 NX44SW 53.01
11	King's Road, Church Hall Development – The demolition site of the Free Kirk and adjoining Church Hall was examined after the building rubble was removed and the wall foundations and underfloor cavity were exposed. The undemolished wall foundations of this site were left undisturbed and covered with fresh sand and gravel.	NX 4459 4018	NX44SW 52
12	King's Road, Cinema – Below the demolition surface of the Cinema in King's Road, a midden of 18th- to 19th-century wine-bottle glass and stoneware pottery was exposed. This overlay a narrow N–S wall base which was plastered on the W face and enclosed a stone and slate floor surface. Below this surface was a stone wall base aligned perpendicular to King's Road. The E end of an earlier building was disturbed by the machine and the rest of it runs W under the back garden of 60 George Street. There was no evidence of earlier occupation below the thin layer of brown soil and stone, contemporary with the midden and earlier building, that spread eastward. There was also evidence of a cobbled surface that was exposed in a small builders' trench, seemingly contemporary with the midden and earlier building. All features overlay natural red boulder clay and/or bedrock.	NX 4461 4018	NX44SW 51.00 and 51.01
13	George Street – A watching brief was carried out on a street lighting cable trench dug up the middle of George Street. At the N end of the trench the full 0.8m depth of the cut was made ground. Part of this digging operation coincided with the former location of a palm tree. The trench cut a series of stones suggestive of wall footings in line with the entrance to St Ninian's Church. The only finds were a few sherds of post-medieval pottery.	NX 4448 4007	NX44SW 82
14	117 George Street – Trial excavation in the living room showed the house to have been built directly upon natural boulder clay. A pit or trench produced 18th- and/or 19th-century bottle glass.	NX 4444 4004	NX44SW 47 NX44SW 171
15	High Street, Town Mill – A small windmill stump at the bottom of Whithorn High Street represents the greatly reduced remains of a much larger tower. The mill derives from the late 18th century, and in a print dated to 1825 displayed in the Priory Museum it appears complete with 4 sails. Undoubtedly this was the town mill and was important to the local population.	NX 4439 3983	NX43NW 30
16	Bruce Street, Museum – A number of sculptural fragments from the Priory, which can be seen in Whithorn Museum, are recorded in NMRS.	NX 4449 4028	NX44SW 56.01 to 56.36
Findspots			
17	'Peter Stone' – A squared stone pillar, 1.2 x 0.4 x 0.25m, bearing an incised cross and inscription stood at this spot in 1872; it was subsequently moved to Whithorn Museum. The inscription, LOCI/PETRI APU/STOLI: 'The place of Peter the Apostle', is written in a style belonging to Merovingian Gaul. This is very rare in Britain, and indicates a 7th-century date.	NX 4431 3921	NX43NW 4
18	Old Town Hall – A perforated hammer of greywacke, found in Whithorn Old Town Hall garden.	NX 4450 4022	NX44SW 18
19	Chapelheron findspot – A stone axe measuring 180mm by 70mm.	NX 4522 4129	NX44SE 5

No.	Name	NGR	NMRS
20	Gallows Outon Cup-and-ring markings – A rock in the vicinity of the spiral-marked rock 350m SSW of Gallows Outon farm, bearing 3 cup-and-ring marks. Now probably turf covered.	NX 4498 4193	NX44SW 36
21	Chapelheron findspot – A Roman coin, sestertius of Faustina I, issued after her death in AD 141, was found on Chapelheron Farm.	NX 455 415	NX44SE 6
22	Whithorn Golf Course Ring-markings – The Rev R S G Anderson reported being shown 'a small fragment of stone in 1927, apparently picked up on the "Duck's Back" green' of Whithorn Golf Course, formerly moorland. He suggested that a mower had possibly chipped it off an outcrop some distance away. This green was about 440m NNE of High Skeog road and 10m W of a wall. The chip was 40mm by 35mm by 10mm. On it were 'two rings and possibly a third'.	NX 452 401	NX44SE 14
	Finds from Whithorn recorded in NMRS (not shown on map, due to imprecise grid references)		
23	Whithorn Golf Course Ring-markings – A slab believed to have been found on the former Whithorn golf course measuring 50mm by 33mm by 100mm. On its flat surface are four concentric rings, 250mm in diameter, and up to 10mm deep.	NX 45 40	NX44SW 15
24	Whithorn – A small 'celt' with rectangular section and finely ground edge, formed of ruddy flint, was found in 1886 near Whithorn.	NX 44 40	NX44SW 17
25	Two stone axes	NX 44 40	NX44SW 16
26	A fragment of a disk-headed cross-slab, comprising the head and part of the shaft, is held by the National Museums of Scotland (IB 35).	NX 44 40	NX44SW 181
27	A fragment of a disk -headed cross -slab, comprising a portion of the cross -head, is held by the National Museums of Scotland (IB 253).	NX 44 40	NX44SW 183
28	A fragment of a disk-headed cross-slab, comprising the cross-head, is held by the National Museums of Scotland (IB 34).	NX 44 40	NX44SW 182
29	A number of Roman and Hiberno-Danish coins were exhibited in Glasgow in 1911. Roman coins have frequently been dug up in the vicinity of Whithorn.	NX 44 40	NX44SW 15
30	The following artefacts from Whithorn are listed by F S E Roe: (i) An asymmetrical mace-head, with flattened ends; (ii) Half of a battle-axe, probably Loose Howe Group; (iii) Half of an ovoid mace-head; (iv) A grooved and dished axe-hammer. Items (i–iii) are in Glasgow Art Galleries and Museum, while (iv) is in the National Museum of Antiquities of Scotland (NMAS)	NX 44 40	NX44SW 19
31	A Roman coin, a small brass of Claudius II (268–69), dug up in 1934.	NX 44 40	NX44SW 8
32	A socketed axe	NX 44 40	NX44SW 46
33	A Roman coin, a brass of Julia Domna (wife of Severus 193–211) was found in 1922 in a garden.	NX 44 40	NX44SW 9

for a building, it assumes this date range. Of its 70-plus Listed Buildings, 25 are ascribed to the late eighteenth century, 23 to *c* 1800, and 17 to the early nineteenth century, leaving barely a handful over. However, a closer look reveals a more complicated story as, for example, the post office at no. 68 George Street, once an inn (the Galloway Arms) (**fig 28**), which retains fine earlier courtyard buildings to the rear. It is listed as being built all of a piece in the later eighteenth or early nineteenth century, but the handsome façade of the later nineteenth-century exposed greywacke with typical red sandstone dressings (probably by the architect William Galloway), has been added to a considerably earlier building, and its pend contains reused priory stonework (**fig 3**).

Some first-generation (medieval) houses in George Street may have had more storeys. There are single-storeyed cylindrical harled outshots in two different locations which look as though they may be remnants of once-higher turnpike staircases going up to now-missing levels. More detailed examination would be able to confirm or refute this. A study of gables and chimney stacks reveals that when a number of buildings were refaced, they were rebuilt a storey or more lower than the original, as appears to be the case, for example, in no. 94 George Street. An unusually thick wall has been noted in no. 100 George Street, and the interiors of both no. 25 and no. 79 George Street, *inter alia*, retain curiosities enough to imply some inheritance from the era of the priory.

It seems likely that the town shrank drastically after the ending of pilgrimage in 1581, a fate unlamented by one *Gazetteer:* 'The overthrow of the traffic of monkery, and the extinction of the factitious attractions of St Ninian's shrine, terminated the social importance of Whithorn, and permanently consigned it to comparative obscurity'.[12] There was little to sustain the town. The regional gentry would have had their town houses in Wigtown, the county town, rather than Whithorn, and Whithorn's own canons would have lived within the monastic precinct. Nonetheless, that raises the question of why the burgh, therefore, had to be so large, and what quality of person would have built a house as grand as the one implied by the doorway to no. 5 George Street (**fig 7**).

Much of the upper town appears to have become depopulated by the end of the sixteenth century. Some indication of the scale of the surviving houses can be obtained from the rather patchy records of the eighteenth-century window tax, but the large level of avoidance associated with this tax makes firm interpretation impossible.[13] In 1748 only five houses in Whithorn were paying the window tax, with another three in the rest of the parish, although by 1758–59 it had risen to 21 houses. The largest, belonging to John Dunlop, writer, had 19 windows, then came the manse (the 'commendator's house') with 14, two houses with 9, two with 8, six with 7, and nine with 6 windows. In 1784–85 only nine houses were paying the tax, eight with 7 windows and one with 11.[14] By contrast, in Wigtown at the same date there were 24 houses, 14 of them with more than 8 windows.[15] In the 1790s, the largest houses in Whithorn were inhabited by a surgeon, a writer and an innkeeper.[16] The records, therefore, seem to show some limited improvement in the overall prosperity of the community, as reflected in its buildings, if the number of windows in taxable houses can be used as a safe indicator of investment and financial security.

The west end of the priory church was restored in the early eighteenth century after the tower collapsed. Further repairs were undertaken in 1734–35, when John Kevan and Alexander Paterson, 'masons in Whithorn', were paid 12s for repairing the burial aisle of the laird of Broughton, which appears to have stood on the south side of the medieval nave, and James Fergussone, 'slater and glazier in Wigtown', was paid £13 6s Scots 'for repairing the kirk of Whithorn in glass and slate-work'.[17] The burgh, therefore, appears to have had competent builders, but lacked specialist architectural craftsmen who had to be brought in from Wigtown. When houses were reoccupied or restored in the later eighteenth century, much old fabric was reused. Yet some of the original rig divisions were split, and two narrow houses created where there may have been only one in earlier times. Particular curiosities of Whithorn are such pairs of narrow houses, with no chimney in their dividing wall, exemplified by nos 112–114 George Street (**fig 46**). Some were subsequently reunited, causing some of the idiosyncrasies apparent today.

Λ comparison of Roy's map of *c* 1750 (**map 3**) with the parliamentary boundaries plan of 1832 (**map 7**) shows that the town had expanded well beyond its medieval boundaries during these eighty years. One hint as to when this happened comes from the statement in the 1830s that 'The dwelling-houses have been much improved since the termination of the war with France, many old ones having been pulled down, and new ones erected on the same site'.[18] Apart from this, the town's recorded history is not particularly helpful in dating its fabric. The parish population expanded at an average of 0.9% per annum between 1755 and 1794, which might suit a first phase of reoccupation, including the cottages on the south-east side of St John Street. However, during the national population spurt between 1794 and 1811, the population of Whithorn rose virtually not at all. In the following decade it surged by 22%, and many of the details – cornices, fanlights, the staircase in no. 29 George Street – appear to be of this date. After that the population dropped slightly, though the number of innkeepers and vintners doubled, to reach a level in 1837 higher than at any other time in the town's recorded history (**table 3**). The town may have been reoccupied, but its state in 1831 remained unimpressive: a burgh lacking trade or manufactures with 'no prospect of any increase'.[19]

The *Report on Municipal Corporations in Scotland* of 1835, summarised in an 1842 *Gazetteer*, emphasised the extent to which Whithorn was not a

FIGURE 46
A house which has been
subdivided (there is no
central chimney stack)
(Paula Martin)

typical burgh: 'there are no burghal taxes; no assessments for the poor; no guildry; no incorporated trades; no exactions of fee for leave to trade within the burgh boundary'.[20] The population of the burgh itself expanded by 15% between 1831 and 1841, and a further 9% between 1841 and 1851 (**table 2**), the *New Statistical Account* of 1839 praising the improved dwelling houses that replaced torn down old fabric. The *Gazetteer* begged leave to differ: 'the houses are slated, and according to the notions that prevailed at the dates of their erection, were originally commodious; but they entirely want regularity of plan, and aggregately suggest – what accords with fact – the idea of an altogether stagnant and probably decaying ancient town'.

The population of the burgh stayed much the same between 1851 and 1881, though that of the parish reduced slightly, and the town reached its largest number of resident gentry in the 1880s (**tables 2 & 3**). The number of masons, wrights and builders remained much the same from 1837 to 1903, suggesting no significant increase in building activity. The characteristic 'modern' facade of Whithorn, with its exposed iron-streaked greywacke, red sandstone margins to doors, and large, almost overscaled, regularly placed windows and ashlar-panelled chimneys, is exemplified in no. 87 George Street, the home of the architect William Galloway (**fig 6**). Galloway, who trained in Edinburgh and at some date was said to have been based in Dumfries, was a historic buildings architect and antiquary who provided many plans for the definitive studies of medieval and post-medieval domestic architecture by MacGibbon and Ross,[21] lithographs of St Magnus Cathedral, Orkney, *inter alia,* and was employed by the Marquess of Bute as the director of the excavations he financed at Whithorn Priory in the 1880s and '90s.[22]

One of the characteristics of his refacing of older buildings is the use of red sandstone that appears to have been shaped to fit (therefore possibly reused from elsewhere), rather than being cut for the purpose. It seems probable that Galloway would have been in a position to retrieve unwanted blocks from the priory as he undertook his work for Bute and, therefore, that these buildings were erected under his influence or design. If that is so, this phase of rebuilding and refacing must date from the mid-1880s until Galloway's death in 1897, though his houses, with their large rectangular windows, were rather anachronistic by that period, and not surprisingly deceived the Historic Buildings Listing Inspectors.

Nineteenth-century expansion largely passed Whithorn by. Even the enormous growth of churches elsewhere in Scotland failed to affect Whithorn. The Roman Catholics only obtained a permanent building in 1960. Two nonconformist churches survive because reused, but of the 1844 Free Kirk there remains only the site.

Both banks (based in the town since the 1840s) moved into purpose-built offices, the Clydesdale in the 1870s (the building being similar to their branch in Stranraer), and the National Bank (now Royal Bank) in 1886 when

FIGURE 47
The new town hall
(Richard Oram)

FIGURE 48
The chimneys of the Black Hawk (Temperance) Hotel
(Richard Oram)

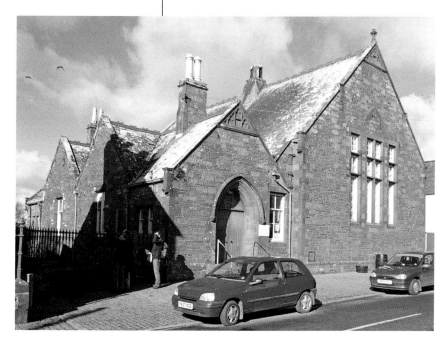

it moved across the road to gabled Scotch baronial premises. The following year the Wigtownshire Railway arrived at the northern edge of the town, and the commercial balance gradually shifted northwards. The town had been creeping north with, for example, the construction of the villa of St Ninian's in 1873, sometimes marooning an earlier farmhouse, like the late eighteenth-century 'The Neuk', in its path, but the railway and associated businesses meant that Victorian modernism, such as it was, came to this part of Whithorn. So, in 1885, a large site was cleared in St John Street for the new town hall designed by the St Andrews' architect David Henry: a Gothic barn with terracotta ridges and simple detailing (**fig 47**).

The previous year, in the same street, the Glasgow architects Thomson and Sandilands had begun their United Presbyterian Church in modern Gothic red sandstone (presumably machine-cut and brought by train from Dumfries), replacing a plain late eighteenth-century Secession Church. Despite conversion to a garage, it still retains some of its stained glass. Into this extended, winding suburban street, another civic building appeared, the Library, designed by Alexander Young in 1911, which presents an over-scaled brick doorway to the street spotted with blue tiles in an echo of Charles Rennie Mackintosh's motifs; and the street was provided with a new guardian at its northern boundary by the Temperance Hotel (**fig 48**). These changes barely dented Whithorn's inherent physical character.

Expansion

One of the outstanding assets of Whithorn is the extent to which it has retained its connection with the surrounding countryside. The backs of the rigs ('back-dykes', as they are termed in other burghs), which extended out from the rear of each street-front property, formed the edge between town and country and, for the most part in Whithorn, they still do. They can best be appreciated on the north-west side, and at the south-western edge between High or Isle Port Mouth and the priory (**fig 7**). The levels of the rigs and their gardens are generally somewhat higher than the countryside beyond, and that provides the edge, but the walls are surprisingly low. Not all rigs are cultivated to the rear, and the condition of the back-dykes merits investment. The edge of the town is largely maintained in the upper town on the east side, except in the southern suburb where twentieth-century house construction has somewhat thoughtlessly breached the skyline.

That hard edge between town and country has broken down, however, to the north and north-east, in the neighbourhood of the railway and the site of the putative castle, as well as in the area of the cow loan to the common grazings (the lane used by cattle avoiding the main street), and to some extent on the road to Portyerrock. On this sunny spot, the town has expanded from 1935 onwards, and the houses reflect the design preoccupations of

FIGURE 49
The side of the Grapes Hotel
(Paula Martin)

the time. Towns have to expand, but most of the construction in this neighbourhood pays scant attention to either the form or the materials of Whithorn's other houses. The adoption of a suburban layout rather than a terraced one has led to the absence of any sense of closure or identity which is so strong elsewhere in the town. If further expansion were to be undertaken in this quarter, it is strongly recommended that it takes a more coherent, space-economic and sheltering form. Equally, the town's identity in this quarter would be greatly assisted by finding new uses not only for The Grapes Hotel (**fig 49**), but also for the buildings running along the back of the rigs forming the boundary of what may have been the back cow loan. Conservation area designation by the council in 1977 ensures that any development must enhance or preserve the character of the area. Proactive management by the local authority, with funding from Historic Scotland, is anticipated through the Conservation Area Regeneration Scheme which is now in preparation, following the successful delivery of a Townscape Heritage Initiative in Wigtown.

Overall assessment

At first sight, Whithorn appears an over-scaled lowland village. In fact it was a valued pilgrimage destination, the form of which survives in its rigs and in some built fabric embedded in standing buildings. It makes little sense at present, since the pilgrimage routes and patterns are neither clear nor fully open, the space dividers that used to shape George Street (the tolbooth and Ket burn) have been removed or disguised, and so little is made of the priory church. The town, however, has enormous charm in the way it folds into the country and the way its boundaries are still delineated by back-dykes to the long rigs. It also has an opportunity to adopt the growing European trend for pilgrimage revival by opening the pilgrimage route to the Isle, re-excavating the priory church and re-presenting it so that its scale might again be appreciated. Other buildings lining the back-dykes of what this survey has called the back cow loan could be repaired and reoccupied, along with those currently without function in the square facing Low Port Mouth. Equally, other neglected rear buildings including the former hostelry courtyard behind the post office could be reoccupied to play a part in any regeneration strategy predicated on heritage tourism.

The physical threats to Whithorn relate to its identity. Pedestrian/traffic conflict in St John Street, for example, could lead to pressure to widen it, but that would destroy the nature of the town. Any expansion to the north-east has to be undertaken with greater sensitivity than heretofore if the compact nature of the town is not to be compromised, and the solecism of the new houses breaching the skyline to the south should not be repeated. The appearance of the town centre would be immeasurably improved by better control of overhead electricity and telephone wires. (Since writing, a programme to fix street lighting to buildings has removed some wiring from the air, so that it now runs instead along the face of buildings. The pros and cons of this enhancement may now be measured.)

Whenever alterations to buildings facing the main street are contemplated, a detailed survey of the fabric would identify whether there is valuable survival of pre-Reformation period features inside. In particular, no. 5 George Street which, from the scale of some of its windows, may be substantially unmodernised and is entered through a remnant of a fine medieval door, deserves detailed recording. The site of the tolbooth in the middle of George Street might be further investigated if the opportunity emerges. At the same time, the buildings at both High and Low Port Mouth should likewise be recorded in detail to determine whether ancient fabric might be contained within them. A complete reconsideration of the priory site is recommended, including the rerouting of the path to the priory church, as part of a plan to revive the original *raison d'être* of Whithorn as a centre of pilgrimage.

Isle of Whithorn (map 13)

Isle of Whithorn was the port of Whithorn and judged, from an early date, to have a good sheltered harbour, though dry at low tide. It did not suffer from the sand, mud or silt that so threatened other harbours further east such as Wigtown and Garlieston. It was where Whithorn's overseas goods (wine and consumables) were landed, where pilgrims disembarked, and also where the stone for the priory church, and maybe other buildings in the town, was landed. Building materials were still being imported from Gothenburg in the mid-eighteenth century, and trade and shipbuilding were at their height in the mid-nineteenth century. Virtually the entire village that exists today in Main Street, Harbour and Tonderghie Road existed in one form or another by 1811.[23] The pilgrimage route to Whithorn began up what is now Portyerrock Road, carrying straight up across what was called the orchard, then over the brae to swing down to enter Whithorn along King's Road.

From its topography, the Isle emerged in several different phases, the first of which, as Pococke observed in 1760, appears to lie in the slightly higher ground where the road leaves northwards of the Drummullin burn for Whithorn. This section of the Isle was almost certainly built-up by the later seventeenth century when Patrick Houston's villa (now Isle Castle) (**fig 50**) was edified or re-edified on elevated ground near the burn in 1674, as evidenced by a reset stone with the date 1674 and the initials of Patrick Houston of Drummaston and his wife Margaret Gordon.[24] The main building is L-plan with a circular stair tower in the re-entrant angle, and its additions appear to be mid-eighteenth- or early nineteenth-century, although they are on the site of the inner court and carry the datestone. Some of the changes may date from when Sir John Reid lived here as Superintendent of the Coastguard *c* 1830, as it was later 'evident that all the [internal] arrangements have been extensively modified to suit modern comfort and convenience'.[25]

Although later called a castle, no contemporary source was thus deceived. It was once a smart house, possibly with a gallery running between its two studies (otherwise turrets) on its top floor, and its carved datestone is no proof whatsoever of its date of origin. It would have been rather anachronistic for that period: one hundred years earlier might be more accurate. Moreover, its inner court lacks buildings such as brewhouse, bakehouse, stables and barn, although the row to the north quite probably formed part of it. It would not be unusual for the house to have been entered from the north, rather than the south, as now, which may have been the location of the privy garden. It is more likely that there was an earlier bridge upstream in the neighbourhood of the mill. What is striking, however, is that the house's architectural detail is not Scots. In place of the normal round Scots corbel to support the projecting corner studies, the detail is of a bracket-corbel of the kind much

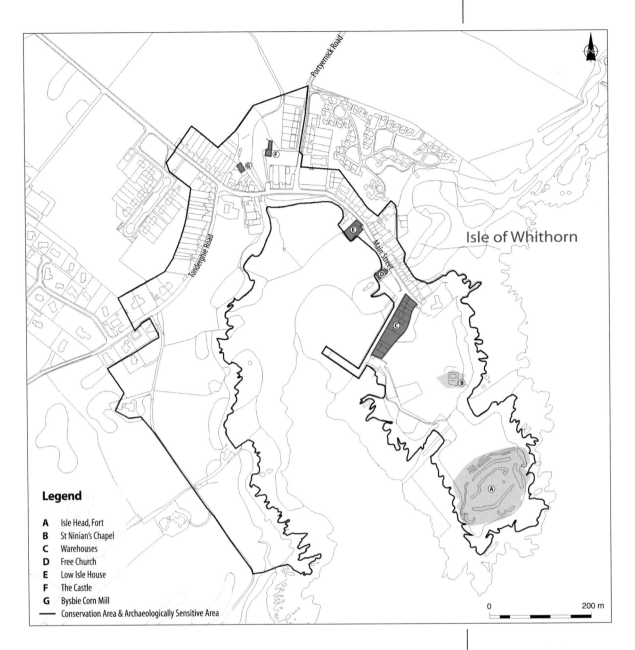

Legend

A   Isle Head, Fort
B   St Ninian's Chapel
C   Warehouses
D   Free Church
E   Low Isle House
F   The Castle
G   Bysbie Corn Mill
—   Conservation Area & Archaeologically Sensitive Area

Isle of Whithorn

Portyerrock Road

Tonderghie Road

Main Street

0   200 m

MAP 13
Isle of Whithorn character
map

FIGURE 50
The 'castle' at Isle of
Whithorn (Colin Martin)

FIGURE 51
The Queen's Arms, Isle of Whithorn. Standing at the
crossroads, it has thick, battered walls, and is probably
older than it looks (Paula Martin)

more common in Ireland. Moreover, the harling lacks any of its likely original brilliance or colour.

The group of buildings around the Queen's Arms hotel, although later eighteenth-century in appearance, seem likely from their strange rear windows and battered plinth to contain older fabric (**fig 51**). In 1759 there were three houses paying window tax. This had dropped to two by 1763 and one the following year.[26] Roy's map of *c* 1750 (**map 4**) and Ainslie's map of 1782 show the island before the causeway was built up. A plan of 1780 (**map 5**) shows the castle standing by the millpond, a few houses to the west and slightly more to the east, but no indication of whether there were more beyond the scope of the plan.[27] Of these handsome two- to two-and-a-half-storeyed houses, none survives as depicted. All those on the east side of the road to Portyerrock were removed, possibly between the wars, when a new community hall and garden were built. A chart of the harbour drawn in 1818 shows elevations of the buildings surrounding the harbour.[28] Most of these are of two storeys, and in much the same positions as today. There are two semicircular areas extending seawards from the road. One is labelled 'carpenter's yard' (where the church now stands), and there are no houses opposite it. The other is the garden of a three-storey house, possibly an inn. It may be this house, rather than the 'castle', which was described in the 1790s as 'a good stone house, on the sea-side' (**fig 52**).[29]

The western projection into the harbour has been extended westwards since the 1818 plan, with a terrace of three houses standing at right angles to the street. On the eastern projection, a simple, rectangular white Free Church was built in 1844, with a handsome bellcote. The houses on Main Street are predominantly substantial two-storeyed painted houses with sturdy chimney stacks, but there are odd idiosyncratic details such as portholes, and

FIGURE 52
House on the seaward side of the street, Isle of Whithorn. The large house and its garden can be seen on the 1818 chart (**map 6**); the terrace has been added later at right angles
(Richard Oram)

the projecting buttress and stones in the wynd that leads to the schoolhouse. Some of the houses have been cut down to a single storey, whereas it is clear from projecting stones that others were originally planned as two-storeyed but never completed. The attraction of these buildings is their scale, and the variety within the homogeneity.[30] Behind them, across the Stinking Port, is the 1970s' holiday-chalet development of Laigh Isle (locally nicknamed 'Toytown'), whose name is considerably more Scottish than either its architecture or its widespread suburban layout (**fig 53**).

The artificial mole, or harbour, is generally said to have been built *c* 1790, but this may refer to the building up of the causeway, as Roy's map of *c* 1750 shows a pier on much the same alignment as today, and the row of buildings along the quayside. The 1818 plan (**map 6**) shows all these as single-storey. The surviving warehouses in their present form therefore must post-date 1818, but 'storehouses' are on record from 1795.[31] A *Gazetteer* of 1842 refers only to 'the few vessels which the unimportant commerce of the district keeps employed'. The harbour was visited by the occasional passenger steamer, but was mainly

FIGURE 53
The 1970s' holiday-home development to the east of Isle of Whithorn (Richard Oram)

used to import coal.[32] The period *c* 1840–80, however, saw an increase in trade, shipping and shipbuilding, and presumably the warehouses were enlarged at this time (**fig 54**). Beneath later warehouse alterations, the rhythm of the original buildings with their granite dressings can be observed.

At the far end of the harbour a footpath leads to the repaired ruins of the presumed thirteenth-century chapel of St Ninian which, apart from its walls, retains almost no credible architectural detail. An excavation of the site in line with the exposed stretch of wall might reveal whether there was indeed a complete boundary wall surrounding the chapel as currently conceived, or whether there were other structures. By 1842 the community was attracting a number of tourists, for 'the weak chalybeate spring', which rises just to the north of Isle Castle, was producing 'waters sufficiently celebrious to draw to the place invalid visitors'; this may have been the start of the Isle's attraction for retired persons.[33] The Isle of Whithorn now presents an obviously

FIGURE 54
Part of the row of
warehouses on the quay at
Isle of Whithorn
(Richard Oram)

picturesque harbour providing excellent views south-west to the Isle of Man. The number of documented nineteenth- and twentieth-century shipwrecks near the entrance to the harbour probably means there is also potential for earlier maritime archaeological sites.[34] It would still be an atmospheric place to land to walk the pilgrimage route to Whithorn. There is more to it than that: the integrated group of buildings comprising the Queen's Arms Hotel, Bysbie mill, the mill-pond beyond, and Isle Castle on the far bank (never mind the chalybeate spring in its gardens) is a very rare survival in a small Scots community, and provides the opportunity for their identification as a significant attraction.

With the exception of Laigh Isle, most contemporary developments in the community have respected its scale and, most important, its natural skyline. The sense of enclosure, however, was ruptured by the demolition of the houses in Main Street between the Portyerrock Road and where Main Street picks up again, probably when the memorial hall and associated garden were built between the wars. The coherence and shelter of the town would be improved if that gap were filled. Otherwise, the scale and skyline represent the most sensitive assets, and any new developments should be assessed in the light of these. Only buildings of great public significance should, in our view, be permitted to breach the skyline. The gap was formed and the Laigh Isle developed before the Conservation Area was designated in 1977, to be extended in 1978 when it was confirmed as outstanding for grants purposes by Historic Scotland. Therefore any future development must preserve or enhance the character of that area. This Burgh Survey may help in suggesting some aspects of that character.

Suggestions for further research

Archaeology

Further investigation would be worthwhile at the following locations in Whithorn:
- ➤ Within the priory church.
- ➤ Outside the north-western end of the priory church.
- ➤ Beneath the path to the parish church through the crossing of the priory.
- ➤ The raised site to the north/north-west of the priory, bounded by the burn.
- ➤ The outer edge of the priory precinct.
- ➤ The boundaries between the priory precinct and the tenements on the west side of George Street.
- ➤ The site of the former tolbooth.
- ➤ The boundaries of tenements on the uphill east side of George Street.
- ➤ The date and nature of backland development in George Street.
- ➤ The site and development of the pre-1800 tolbooth.
- ➤ The site of the windmill.
- ➤ Buildings which appear to contain older fabric (eg no. 5 George Street).

Further investigation would be worthwhile at the following location in Isle of Whithorn:
- ➤ The area between the mill and Isle Castle and the chalybeate well, and a possible bridge at that point.

History

In terms of historical research, the following questions remain to be answered:
- ➤ The activities and relationship of William Galloway and the Marquess of Bute.
- ➤ The relationship between Whithorn and the rural hinterland of the parish.
- ➤ The relationship – both social and architectural – between Whithorn and Ireland.

> The relationship – both social and architectural – between Whithorn, the Isle of Man and north-western England.
> The relationship between the great regional families and Whithorn.
> The relationship between the local lairdly families and Whithorn.
> The local impact of improvement agriculture in the eighteenth and nineteenth centuries.

Notes

1 Its footings were relocated during a watching brief on a pipeline trench at NX 4448 4007 (NMRS no. NX44SW 82) in 2001

2 Pococke, *Tour*, 14

3 *OSA*, 533

4 Symson, *Galoway*, 46

5 *Sasine Abridgements, Wigtownshire*, a sasine dated 3 March 1849 mentions the 'Green of Whithorn, being part of the Windmill Hill'

6 It is listed in *Slater's Directory* in 1882 but not in 1878

7 The original church at Dryburgh Abbey appears to have been conceived on a grander scale and had a nave with aisles, in contrast to the aisleless arrangement at Whithorn, but financial crisis prevented Dryburgh's plan from ever being fully realised. See Fawcett and Oram, *Dryburgh Abbey*

8 NMRS record NX44SW 51.01 (information from Jane Brann, Dumfries and Galloway Planning & Environment Services), the cinema stood on the south side of King's Road, opposite the Belmont Hall

9 NMRS record NX44SW 53.01

10 *DES*, 2003

11 Nicholson 1999, Intervention D. The longer rigs are on the east side of George Street. This is said to be because the soil is better. It is black, and said to derive from ships' ballast (though many old burghs have deep black soil in their backlands). Locals told us that those who live on that side tend to win the prizes for vegetables

12 *The Topographical, Statistical and Historical Gazetteer of Scotland* (Glasgow, 1842), ii, 805

13 It is common throughout history for new taxes to have a high return, and then the income to drop as avoidance measures are identified (or corruption sets in), see for example T Scrase, *Somerset Towns: changing fortunes 800–1800* (Stroud, 2005), 24, '... the standard problem encountered when working with tax records. It is whether observed changes show real alterations in wealth or population or instead reflect changes in the behaviour of one or more of government, the tax assessors, the tax collectors, and the taxpayers. The classical case is the contrast between the 1377 poll tax and its successors. Apparent populations crumbled'

14 NAS E326/123. Over the years the categories changed, and possibly the definition of a window changed, as the number of houses paying the tax shrank to 19 in 1760, 18 in 1762, 16 in 1763, 15 the following year, reducing

to 11 by 1769–70, the lowest count being 8 in 1777–78. It then rose to 24 ten years later. The numbers of windows Dunlop was charged for varied from 19 to 14 to 11 to 7. The manse dropped from 14 to 9 to 7, then rose to 16 again. The minister, Mr Adair, and John Dunlop, were the only two inhabitants to pay the Inhabited House Tax in 1786–87, NAS E326/63

15 NAS E326/218

16 The tax lists do not normally give the occupations of those paying, but occasionally they do, or occupational data can be derived from other sources

17 NAS GD10/583

18 *NSA*, 54

19 *Report on boundaries, 1832*

20 *Report on Municipal Corporations*, 429; *Topographical, Statistical and Historical Gazetteer*, ii, 803

21 MacGibbon, D and Ross, T, *The Castellated and Domestic Architecture of Scotland*, 5 vols (Edinburgh, 1887–92)

22 A William Galloway was a witness to the will of the architect James Gillespie Graham, and the dates fit for our WG to have been a trainee in Gillespie's office. According to D Walker, *Dictionary of Scottish Architects* online, Galloway had an office in Dumfries, but no evidence could be found in Directories from 1867 onwards for Galloway as an architect in either Whithorn or Dumfries, so presumably he was not in practice but working full-time for the Marquess of Bute. But he does seem the most likely candidate to have been responsible for much of the refacing of houses in Whithorn

23 NAS RHP42253

24 Datestones are very tricky since they can be inserted at any time, and can be moved from building to building; this datestone cannot be used as a reliable date for the construction of Isle Castle

25 MacGibbon and Ross, *The Castellated and Domestic Architecture of Scotland*, v, 354–6

26 NAS E326/215

27 NAS RHP663

28 NAS RHP42253

29 *OSA*, 552

30 A large and picturesquely undulating timber-framed boatbuilding shed which added to the character of this area has recently been demolished

31 NAS GD455/53

32 *Topographical, Statistical and Historical Gazetteer*, ii, 58

33 *Topographical, Statistical and Historical Gazetteer*, ii, 58

34 P C Miller, *Galloway Shipwrecks* (Stranraer, 1992)

Glossary

ashlar	Squared and dressed hewn stone used for building purposes.
bailie	The top councillors were provost, bailies (usually between two and four), treasurer and Dean of Guild. These 'magistrates' ran the town on a day-to-day basis, called council meetings etc.
barony	The land or lands controlled by a baron.
burgage	A form of tenure by which lands or tenements in burghs were held of a superior for an annual rent; the tenements held under that tenure.
burgess	Member of the core of craftsmen and merchants within a burgh, who had exclusive privileges within the burgh. Membership could be inherited, acquired by marriage to a burgess's daughter, or purchased.
burgh of barony	A town founded and controlled by a baron, by means of a grant from the monarch.
burgh of regality	Similar to a burgh of barony, but with more royal powers delegated to the baron.
cairn	Pile of stones, sometimes covering a prehistoric burial.
campanile	Bell tower
canon	A priest living in common with other priests and following a rule of monastic life, usually that drawn up by St Augustine (Augustinian) or St Norbert (Premonstratensians). Also, a priest ordering his life according to the canons of the church, often being a member of an ecclesiastical chapter.
chamberlain	An officer, originally with oversight of the private chambers of the king or a great lord, later serving as chief financial officer, receiver of rents etc.
charter	Formal legal document, usually issued by the crown or a superior lord, detailing the properties, rights and obligations of the recipient.
commendator	An individual holding an important ecclesiastical benefice, with the right to enjoy its revenues, but not installed as titular holder of the benefice. Possession could be for life or until a permanent incumbent was installed.

common good	The lands or other sources of income which were held and managed by a burgh on behalf of its inhabitants.
diocese	The territory under the jurisdiction of a bishop.
feretory	A receptacle to hold the relics of saints (a reliquary)/ an area of a church in which reliquaries are kept
feu	Grant of land rights. In exchange for a fixed sum and a continued fixed annual rent, a tenant bought the right to hold a property in perpetuity, and to bequeath or sell it.
foreland	Land in front of a house which belongs to the house, and could be used for any purpose, including middens. For this reason owners were encouraged to give them up to become a part of the public pavement, or to rebuild the house further forward. But in many towns a few remain, as at the west side of the top end of George Street.
guildry	Merchant guild, entered by family links or purchase, with exclusive rights to trade within the liberties of a burgh.
Hagbutter	Footsoldier bearing an early firearm, the arquebus, derived from German *haken* to hook, and *busse* gun, as it had to be hooked on to a support.
harling	The traditional coating for rubble stone walls in Scotland, whether high-status or vernacular, both as a protection from the weather and to create the impression of geometric mass. Formed from a mixture of local aggregate bound with lime.
infeft	Technical term for the process by which an individual is given possession of property or rights by a superior lord.
liberty	The area within which a burgh had exclusive trading rights. As more burghs were created, they inevitably impinged on the liberties of earlier ones.
merk	A medieval unit of account equivalent to 13 shillings and 4d or two-thirds of a pound sterling.
merkland	Scots measure of the worth or area of a piece of land. Rent was traditionally paid in kind rather than cash, and the merk was one of the units of value. A merkland was a unit of land productivity.
mesolithic	Of the middle Stone Age, the earliest period of prehistoric settlement in Scotland. Mesolithic people were nomadic hunter-gatherers, using fine stone tools.

midden	Rubbish heap, whether domestic, agricultural or mixed.
multivallate	Surrounded by several banks and diches.
patronage	The right of appointment. The right of landowners to appoint ministers of the Church of Scotland had long been contentious, and eventually led to the Disruption in 1843.
provost	The head of the chapter of a collegiate church; the chief magistrate of a burgh.
quire	The eastern portion of a church occupied by the clergy and choir, also referred to as 'the choir'.
regality	Lands and associated rights of jurisdiction where the landlord exercised all rights and legal powers usually associated with the crown – except the right to try treason cases – and where authority of royal justiciars and sheriffs did not operate. Abolished in 1747.
royal burgh	A burgh which paid taxes direct to the crown in exchange for the right to self-government, and whose rights included foreign trade.
sasine	The act of taking possession of a property, symbolised by the handing over of an object (eg a piece of turf from the land in question), and recorded in a document called a sasine.
Scotch Baronial	Victorian architectural style alluding to sixteenth-/seventeenth-century Franco-Scots Renaissance architecture, characterised by crow steps, turrets and bartizans.
skew	Sloping stones that cap a gable and stop the roof.
skewputt	Large stone where the skew meets the wallhead, often treated in a local decorative style.
stent	Local tax, assessed on the value of landed property
teind	The tenths of produce (in England, tithes) rendered by parishioners for the upkeep of the local priest and church.
tenement	Land or real property held of another by any form of tenure; in Scotland a large building let in portions to a number of tenants.
thackstane	A stone projecting from the chimney, to stop water running down the chimney and getting under thatch. Sometimes persisted even where not thatched.
thirlage	Obligation on tenants to have their corn ground only

	in the estate mill.
tolbooth	The central administrative building of a burgh, usually combining council and court rooms, weigh house and prison.
vennel	A narrow passage or lane between buildings, usually in a burgh.

Bibliography

Primary sources

NAS CC8/8/90

NAS CC22/3/4B and 5A

NAS E326/15/31, Consolidated Taxes

NAS E326/63, Inhabited House Tax

NAS E326/123, 215, 218, Window Tax

NAS GD10/221

NAS GD10/583

NAS GD10/1299

NAS GD18, Clerk of Penicuik Papers

    GD18/2215, letter of thanks to Clerk, as Baron of Exchequer, for 100 merks towards steeple and bell, 19/01/1709, and receipt 04/02/09

    GD18/3128, Copy Minute Book of the Commissioners of Parliament for examination of public accounts, 1703–1704

NAS GD30/393

NAS GD30/586

NAS GD30/610

NAS GD30/936

NAS GD30/1967

NAS GD455/15/5

NAS GD455/53

NAS SC19/41, sheriff court, testaments (via ScotlandsPeople.gov.uk)

Maps and plans

Maps C.9.b, William Roy, Military Survey of Scotland, 1747–55, 1:36,000, sheet 03/7e

NAS RHP663, 'Plan of the orchard of Isle of Whithorn', 1780

NAS RHP42253, 'The Harbour of Whithorn', 1818

Ordnance Survey, 1:10,560, first edition, 1849; second edition 1894; third edition 1903 (dates of survey)

Report upon the boundaries of the several cities burghs and towns of Scotland, 1832, map of Parliamentary boundary of Whithorn

Printed primary sources

A Diurnal of Remarkable Occurrents That Have Passed Within the Country of Scotland Since the Death of King James IV till the Year 1575 (Bannatyne Club, 1833)

Accounts of the Lord High Treasurer of Scotland, i, 1473–1498, T Dickson (ed) (Edinburgh, 1877)

Accounts of the Lord High Treasurer of Scotland, ii, 1500–1504, J Balfour Paul (ed) (Edinburgh, 1900)

Accounts of the Lord High Treasurer of Scotland, iii, *1506–1507*, J Balfour Paul (ed) (Edinburgh, 1901)

Accounts of the Lord High Treasurer of Scotland, iv, *1507–1513*, J Balfour Paul (ed) (Edinburgh, 1902)

Accounts of the Lord High Treasurer of Scotland, vi, *1515–1531*, J Balfour Paul (ed) (Edinburgh, 1903)

Calendar of Documents Relating to Scotland, ii, *1272–1307*, J Bain (ed) (Edinburgh, 1884)

Calendar of Documents Relating to Scotland, v, *1108–1516* (Supplementary), G G Simpson and J D Galbraith (eds) (Edinburgh, 1985)

Calendar of Entries in the Papal Registers Relating to Great Britain and Ireland: Papal Letters, xii, 1458–1471, J A Twemlow (ed) (London, 1933)

Calendar of Scottish Supplications to Rome 1428–1432, A I Dunlop and I B Cowan (eds) (SHS, 1970)

Calendar of Scottish Supplications to Rome, iv, *1433–1447*, A I Dunlop and D MacLauchlan (eds) (Glasgow, 1983)

Calendar of State Papers Relating to Scotland and Mary, Queen of Scots 1547–1603, iii, *1569–1571*, W K Boyd (ed) (Edinburgh, 1903)

Calendar of State Papers Relating to Scotland and Mary, Queen of Scots 1547–1603, iv, *1571–1574*, W K Boyd (ed) (Edinburgh, 1905)

Calendar of State Papers Relating to Scotland and Mary, Queen of Scots 1547–1603, x, *1589–1593*, W K Boyd and H W Meikle (eds) (Edinburgh, 1936)

A Directory of Landownership in Scotland c 1770, L R Timperley (ed) (Scottish Record Society, 1976)

Dumfries Weekly Journal

The Exchequer Rolls of Scotland, J Stuart *et al* (eds) (Edinburgh, 1878–1908)

Fasti Ecclesiae Scoticanae Medii Aevi ad Annum 1638, D E R Watt (ed) (Scottish Record Society, 1969)

The Heads of Religious Houses in Scotland from Twelfth to Sixteenth Centuries, D E R Watt and N F Shead (eds) (Scottish Record Society, 2001)

Historians of the Church of York and Its Archbishops, J Raine (ed), 2 vols (London, 1869–94)

History of the Union of Scotland and England by Sir John Clerk of Pennicuik, D Duncan (trans and ed) (SHS, 1993)

Legends of the Saints in the Scots Dialect of the Fourteenth Century, W M Metcalfe (ed), iii (Edinburgh, 1891)

The Legends of SS Ninian and Machor, W M Metcalfe (ed) (Edinburgh, 1904)

Njal's Saga, M Magnusson and H Pálsson (trans.) (Harmondsworth, 1960)

Pigot and Co's New Commercial Directory of Scotland for 1825–26 (London and Manchester)

Pococke, *Tour through Scotland, 1760*, D W Kemp (ed) (SHS, 1887)

Poor Law Inquiry Commission for Scotland (1844), Examinations, Synod of Galloway, Parish of Whithorn, 529

Records of the Convention of the Royal Burghs of Scotland, iii, 1614–1676 (Edinburgh, 1878)

Records of the Convention of the Royal Burghs of Scotland, iv, 1677–1711 (Edinburgh, 1880)

Regesta Regum Scotorum, v, *The Acts of Robert I*, A A M Duncan (ed) (Edinburgh, 1988)

Regesta Regum Scotorum, vi, *The Acts of David II*, B Webster (ed) (Edinburgh, 1976)

Register of John le Romeyn, Lord Archbishop of York (Surtees Society, 1913–16)

Register of the Privy Council of Scotland, ii, *1569–1578*, J H Burton (ed) (Edinburgh, 1878)

Register of the Privy Council of Scotland, vi, *1599–1604*, D Masson (ed) (Edinburgh, 1884)

Register of the Privy Council of Scotland, xi, *1616–1619*, D Masson (ed) (Edinburgh, 1894)

Register of the Privy Council of Scotland, 2nd ser, i, *1625–1627*, D Masson (ed) (Edinburgh, 1899)

Register of the Privy Council of Scotland, 3rd ser, iii, *1669–1672*, P Hume Brown (ed) (Edinburgh, 1910)

Register of the Privy Council of Scotland, 3rd ser, viii, *1683–1684*, P Hume Brown (ed) (Edinburgh, 1915)

Register of the Privy Seal of Scotland, vii, *1575–1580*, G Donaldson (ed) (Edinburgh, 1966)

Register of the Privy Seal of Scotland, viii, *1581–1584*, G Donaldson (ed) (Edinburgh, 1982)

'Register Containing the State and Condition of every Burgh within the Kingdom of Scotland … 1692', in *Miscellany of the Scottish Burgh Records Society* (Edinburgh, 1881)

Register of Walter Gray, Lord Archbishop of York, J Raine (ed) (Surtees Society, 1870)

Registrum Magni Sigilli Regum Scotorum, i, *1306–1424*, J M Thomson (ed) (repr. Edinburgh, 1984)

Registrum Magni Sigilli Regum Scotorum, ii, *1424–1513*, J Balfour Paul (ed) (repr. Edinburgh, 1984)

Report from Select Committee on Orange Institutions in Great Britain and the Colonies (1835)

Report upon the boundaries of the several cities burghs and towns of Scotland … 1832

Report on Municipal Corporations in Scotland (1835)

Sasine Abridgements, Wigtownshire

Slater's Directories for 1837, 1852, 1860, 1867, 1873, 1878, 1882, 1886, 1889, 1893, 1900, 1903, 1907, 1911, 1915 (Manchester and London)

The Statistical Account of Scotland 1791–1799: vol. 1, General, D J Withrington and I R Grant (eds) (Wakefield, 1983)

The Statistical Account of Scotland 1791–1799: vol. 5, Stewartry of Kirkcudbright and Wigtownshire, D J Withrington and I R Grant (eds) (Wakefield, 1983), 'Parish of Whithorn', Rev Isaac Davidson, 1794

The Statistical Account of Scotland (Edinburgh, 1845), 'Parish of Whithorn', Rev Christopher Nicholson, 1839

Smith, Samuel, *General View of the Agriculture of Galloway* (London, 1810)

Symson, Andrew, *A Large Description of Galoway by Andrew Symson, Minister of Kirkinner, 1684* (Edinburgh, 1823)

Third Statistical Account of Scotland, The County of Wigtown, M C Arnott (ed) (Glasgow, 1965), parish of Whithorn, Rev John Scoular, 1952 and 1962)

Turner, Sir James, *Memoirs of His Own Life and Times, MDCXXXII–MDCLXX* (Bannatyne Club, 1829)

Webster, J, *General View of the Agriculture of Galloway* (Edinburgh, 1794)

Wigtownshire Charters, R C Reid (ed) (SHS, 1960)

Secondary sources

Ashley, A, 'Odo, Elect of Whithern, 1235', *TDGNHAS*, 3rd ser, xxxvii (1958–59), 62–9

Aspinwall, B, 'The Making of the Modern Diocese of Galloway', in McCluskey (ed) 1997, 81–190

The Book of Galloway 1745, reprinted from the *Galloway Gazette* (Newton Stewart, 1912)

Brentano, R J, 'Whithorn and York', *SHR* (1953), 144–6

Brentano, R J, 'The Whithorn Vacancy', *Innes Review*, iv (1953), 71–83

Brooke, D, *The Medieval Cult of St Ninian* (Friends of the Whithorn Trust, 1988)

Brooke, D, 'The Northumbrian Settlements in Galloway and Carrick: an Historical Assessment', *PSAS*, **121** (1991), 295–327

Campbell, R H, *Owners and Occupiers: Changes in Rural Society in South-West Scotland before 1914* (Aberdeen, 1991)

Cannon, J, *Droll Recollections of Whithorn and Vicinity* (Dumfries, 1904)

Chadburn, R, 'Building stone sources for Whithorn Priory, Dundrennan Abbey and other historic sites in Galloway', *TDGNHAS*, lxxxi (2007), 63–70

Checkland, S G, *Scottish Banking: a history 1695–1973* (Glasgow & London, 1975)

Clark, G, 'Rural Land Use from *c* 1870', in G Whittington and I Whyte, *An Historical Geography of Scotland* (London, 1983)

Clarke, A, *Whithorn 7. Interim Report on the 1995 and 1996 Excavations at Whithorn Priory* (The Whithorn Trust, 1997)

Cooke, G A, *Topographical Description of Scotland*, Southern Scotland (London, *c* 1805)

Craig, D, 'Pre-Norman Sculpture in Galloway: Some Territorial Implications', in Oram and Stell 1991, 45–62

Cullen, L M, 'Incomes, social classes and economic growth in Ireland and Scotland, 1600–1900', in T M Devine and D Dickson (eds), *Ireland and Scotland 1600–1850* (Edinburgh, 1983), 248–60

Devine, T M, *The Scottish Nation 1700–2000* (London, 1999)

Dick, C H, *Highways and Byways in Galloway and Carrick* (London, 1916)

Dilworth, M, *Scottish Monasteries in the Late Middle Ages* (Edinburgh, 1995)

Donnachie, I, 'The Economy of Galloway in Historical Perspective', in *The Galloway Project: a Study of the Economy of South West Scotland with Particular Reference to its Tourist Potential* (Scottish Tourist Board, Edinburgh, 1968)

Donnachie, I, *The Industrial Archaeology of Galloway* (Newton Abbot, 1971)

Donnachie, I, and MacLeod, I, *Old Galloway* (Newton Abbot, 1974)

Dumfries and Galloway Through the Lens, 2, Glimpses of Old Whithorn (Dumfries, 1997)

Dumfries and Galloway Through the Lens, 16, Glimpses of Old Whithorn and Glasserton parishes (Dumfries, 1999)

Dumfries and Galloway Through the Lens, 18, Glimpses of old Galloway Seaports (Dumfries, 2000)

Durkan, J, 'The sanctuary and college of Tain', *Innes Review*, xiii (1962), 147–56

Easson, D E, *Medieval Religious Houses: Scotland* (London, 1957)

Evans, J, Palmer, E, and Walter, R (eds), *A Harbour Goes to War: the story of Mulberry and the men who made it happen* (Garlieston, *c* 2000)

Ewart, G, *Cruggleton Castle* (Dumfries, 1986)

Faed, James (artist) and Sloan J M (descriptive text), *Galloway* (London, 1908)

Fawcett, R, and Oram, R D, *Melrose Abbey* (Stroud, 2004)

Fawcett, R, and Oram, R D, *Dryburgh Abbey* (Stroud, 2005)

Fraser, A, *Mary Queen of Scots* (London, 1969)

Fraser, G, *Lowland Lore; or the Wigtownshire of long ago* (Wigtown, 1880)

Gifford, J, *The Buildings of Scotland: Dumfries and Galloway* (London, 1996)

Groome, F, *Ordnance Gazetteer* (Glasgow, 1894–95)

Handley, J E, *The Irish in Scotland 1798–1845* (Cork, 1945)

Harper, M M, *Rambles in Galloway*, 3rd edn (Dumfries, 1908)

Hill, P, *Whithorn and St Ninian. The Excavation of a Monastic Town, 1984–91* (The Whithorn Trust & Sutton Publishing, Stroud, 1997)

Jones, H C, *The Wigtownshire Hearth Tax Collection Lists of 1692* (Greenbrook, Australia, 1979)

Lenman, B, *The Jacobite Risings in Britain 1689–1746* (Aberdeen, 1980)

MacGibbon, D, and Ross, T, *The Castellated and Domestic Architecture of Scotland*, 5 vols (Edinburgh, 1887–92)

MacGibbon, D, and Ross, T, *The Ecclesiastical Architecture of Scotland*, 3 vols (Edinburgh, 1896–97)

Mackay, D, 'The Four Heid Pilgrimages of Scotland', *Innes Review*, xix (1968)

MacQueen, J, 'The Literary Sources for the Life of St Ninian', in Oram and Stell 1991, 17–25

McCluskey, R (ed), *The See of Ninian: A History of the Medieval Diocese of Whithorn and the Diocese of Galloway in Modern Times* (Ayr, 1997)

McCluskey, R, 'Introduction: celebrating St Ninian', in McCluskey (ed) 1997, 1–20

M'Kerlie, P H, *History of the Lands and their Owners in Galloway*, 2 vols (Edinburgh, 1870, reprinted ed. Gardner, Paisley, 1906)

Maclennan, M, *A Pronouncing and Etymological Dictionary of the Gaelic Language* (repr. Aberdeen, 1988)

MacLeod, I, *Discovering Galloway* (Edinburgh, 1986)

Miller, P C, *Galloway Shipwrecks* (Stranraer, 1992)

Morris, J, *An Illustrated Guide to our Lifeboat Stations, 7, Scotland* (privately published, nd)

Morrison, I, 'Galloway: Locality and Landscape Evolution', in Oram and Stell 1991, 13–14

Munn, C W, *Clydesdale Bank: the first hundred years* (London and Glasgow, 1988)

Murchie, A T, *The Mulberry Harbour Project in Wigtownshire in 1942–1944* (Wigtown, 1993)

Official Guide to the Royal Burgh of Whithorn issued by authority of Whithorn Town Council (Newton Stewart, *c* 1950)

Oram, R D, 'Bruce, Balliol and the lordship of Galloway', *TDGNHAS*, 3rd ser, lxvii (1992), 29–47

Oram, R D, 'Scandinavian settlement in south-west Scotland with a special study of Bysbie', in B E Crawford (ed.), *Scandinavian Settlement in Northern Britain* (London, 1995), 127–40

Oram, R D, 'Heirs to Ninian: the medieval bishops of Whithorn (*circa* 1100–1560)', in McCluskey (ed) 1997, 49–80

Oram, R D, 'Dervorgilla, the Balliols and Buittle', *TDGNHAS*, 3rd ser, lxxiii (1999), 165–81

Oram, R D, *The Lordship of Galloway* (Edinburgh, 2000)

Oram, R D, 'Introduction: an Overview of the Reign of Alexander II', in R D Oram (ed), *The Reign of Alexander II* (Leiden, 2005), 1–48

Oram, R D, *A Monastery and its Landscape: Whithorn and Monastic Estate Management in Galloway (c 1250–c 1600): 13th Whithorn Lecture* (Friends of the Whithorn Trust, 2005)

Oram, R D, and Stell, G (eds), *Galloway: Land and Lordship* (Edinburgh, 1991)

Oram, R D, Martin, P F, McKean, C A, Cathcart, A, and Neighbour, T, *Historic Tain. Archaeology and development* (York, 2009)

Philip, L J, 'Planned villages in Dumfries and Galloway 1730–1850', *Scottish Geographical Journal* **119**.2 (2003), 77–98

Pollock, D, *Whithorn 5. Interim Report on the 1992 Excavations at Whithorn Priory* (The Whithorn Trust, 1993)

Pollock, D, *Whithorn 6. Interim Report on the 1993 Excavations at Whithorn Priory* (The Whithorn Trust, 1995)

Ralegh Radford, C A, 'Cruggleton Church', *TDGNHAS*, 3rd ser, xxviii (1949–50), 92–5

Ralegh Radford, C A, 'Excavations at Whithorn (Final Report)', *TDGNHAS*, 3rd ser, xxxiv (1955–56), 131–94

Ralegh Radford, C A, 'The Churches of Dumfriesshire and Galloway', *TDGNHAS*, 3rd scr, xl (1961–62), 102–16

Ralegh Radford, C A, and Donaldson, G, *Whithorn and Kirkmadrine* (HMSO, 1953)

Ralegh Radford, C A, and Donaldson, G, *Whithorn and the Ecclesiastical Monuments of Wigtown District* (Edinburgh, 1984)

Romantic Galloway. Guide and Holiday Brochure for South West Scotland (Castle Douglas, 1954)

Royal Commission on the Ancient and Historical Monuments of Scotland, *Tolbooths and Townhouses: Civic Architecture in Scotland to 1833* (HMSO, 1996)

Russell, J A, *The Book of Galloway* (Dumfries, 1962)

Scrase, T, *Somerset Towns: changing fortunes 800–1800* (Stroud, 2005)

Smith, D L, *The Little Railways of South-West Scotland* (Newton Abbot, 1969)

Smout, T C, *Scottish Trade on the Eve of Union, 1660–1707* (Edinburgh, 1963)

Smyth, A P, *Warlords and Holy Men: Scotland AD 80–1000* (London, 1984)

Taylor, W, *The Military Roads in Scotland* (Newton Abbot, 1976)

Thomas, C, *Whithorn's Christian Beginnings. First Whithorn Lecture 19th September 1992* (Friends of the Whithorn Trust, 1992)

Thomson, D, *226 Heavy Anti-Aircraft Battery 1939–1945: a personal account of the Caithness and Orkney battery* (Kirkwall, 1995)

Toolis, R, 'A survey of the promontory forts of the North Solway coast', *TDGNHAS* **77**, 2003, 37–78

The Topographical, Statistical and Historical Gazetteer of Scotland (Glasgow, 1842)

Veitch, K, 'The conversion of native religious communities to the Augustinian Rule in twelfth- and thirteenth-century Alba', *Records of the Scottish Church History Society*, xxix (1999), 1–22

Walker, G, 'The Protestant Irish in Scotland', in T M Devine (ed), *Irish Immigrants and Scottish Society in the Nineteenth and Twentieth Centuries* (Edinburgh, 1991), 44–66

Whatley, C A, 'Taking Stock: Scotland at the End of the Seventeenth Century', in T C Smout (ed), *Anglo-Scottish Relations from 1603 to 1900* (Oxford, 2005), 103–25

Yeoman, P, *Pilgrimage in Medieval Scotland,* Historic Scotland (London, 1999)

Unpublished Sources

Birchman, J E, 'Old Kirkyard, Whithorn' (typescript list of monumental inscriptions, nd)

Harrington, P, 'Scottish Power's Electricity Pole and Stave Block Trenches, Whithorn' (unpublished report for Dumfries and Galloway SMR, 1992)

Lowe, C, 'Early Ecclesiastical Enclosures at Whithorn: an archaeological assessment' (unpublished report, Headland Archaeology Ltd, 2001)

Martin, P, 'Cupar, Fife, 1700–*c* 1820, a small Scottish town in an era of change' (unpublished PhD thesis, University of Dundee, 2000)

Morrison, J, 'An Archaeological Evaluation at Whithorn, Dumfries & Galloway' (unpublished report, Headland Archaeology Ltd, 2001)

Morrison, J, 'Research and Training Excavation in the Manse Field, Whithorn, Dumfries & Galloway: Data Structure Report' (unpublished report, Headland Archaeology Ltd, 2003)

Nicholson, A, 'Whithorn Watching Brief: November 1998/January 1999' (unpublished report by Wigtownshire Archaeology Associates for British Telecom, 1999)

Oram, R D, 'Torhousemuir Historical Account. Report on a Programme of Research undertaken by Retrospect Historical Services on Behalf of Scottish Natural Heritage' (1995)

Ramsay, S, Miller, J, and Housely, R, 'Whithorn Environs: Palaeoenvironmental Investigation of Rispain Mire' (First draft. Dept of Archaeology, University of Glasgow, nd)

Scoular, A, 'Tourism in the Whithorn area of South West Scotland' (unpublished undergraduate dissertation, Dept of Geography, University of St Andrews, 1994)

Index

NB: numbers in **bold** refer to figures or their captions